Uniforms of the Armies at Waterloo

Volume 1
The British Army

As Drawn by
Charles Lyall
1894

Authors:	Markus Gärtner & Markus Stein
Translation:	Richard Sanders
Advisor:	Lutz Amsel
Layout:	Stefan Müller
Publisher:	Zeughaus Verlag GmbH Knesebeckstr. 88, 10623 Berlin
Phone:	+49 (0)30-315-700-30
Fax:	+49 (0)30-315-700-77
Email:	info@zeughausverlag.de
Internet:	www.zeughausverlag.de

Printed in European Union, 2024

All rights reserved.
Reproductions, translation, photographic reproduction, including extracts, are forbidden. Storage and distribution including transfer onto electronic media like CD-ROM etc. as well as storage on electronic media like the Internet etc. are not permissible without the express written permission of the publisher and are punishable.

© Zeughaus Verlag GmbH, Berlin 2024
ISBN: 978-3-96360-003-6

INTRODUCTION

For the first time, a previously unpublished work of the British uniform painter Charles Lyall is presented to the general public. In parts of his drawing work, the artist tried to show the troops of the 1815 campaign. Lyall presented the soldiers and officers of the armies involved in the last campaign of the Napoleonic Wars in numerous watercolour illustrations.

In producing the plates, Charles Lyall focused on using the sources that were available at his time, some of which originated during the Napoleonic Wars. Also, if the paintings do not have any explicit reference to the underlying sources, the origin can be deduced from the stances of the figures as well as attributed to artistic license.

This "The Armies at Waterloo" publication is based on the structure of Lyall's work, so it is divided into the following four volumes:

1. The British Army of 1815 with 74 plates
2. The Allied Forces of 1815 with troops from the Netherlands, Hanover (including the King's German Legion), Nassau and Brunswick with 56 plates
3. The Prussian Army of 1815 with 39 plates
4. The French Army of 1815 with 70 plates

All the plates are published with brief remarks about the deployment of the units in the 1815 campaign, especially at the decisive battle of Waterloo, as well as about the depicted uniforms, equipment and weapons. These remarks are intended to allow a critical classification of the depicted soldiers according to what is currently known about the uniforms of this era. The unit strengths mentioned in the comments are based on the numbers compiled by Mark Adkin in his "Waterloo Companion" for June 18th, 1815. A brief introduction to the soldiers' and officers' uniforms accompanies the plates and allows the reader to get a picture of the appearance of the troops.

A comprehensive historical account of the campaign of 1815 is intentionally omitted, as the authors seek to limit the work to the appearance of the participating armies. Nevertheless, in order to get the military historical context, the four volumes are published using maps from the rare atlas in Siborne's work. The detailed map of the Battle of Waterloo in this volume is followed by Quatre-Bras in the second volume, the battle of Ligny and Wavre in the third, and another two maps of the Battle of Waterloo in the fourth volume. The maps are supplemented with brief summaries of the events in the 1815 campaign.

At the end of each volume a selected bibliography with relevant and recent works on military history and uniforms is provided to allow more extensive research.

Markus Gärtner & Markus Stein

**Charles Lyall as an opera singer in
"The Lily of Killarney"**
*(From the collection of Kurt Gänzl,
author of "Victorian Vocalists")*

Charles Lyall and the "Armies of Waterloo"

Identifying the artist Charles Lyall had been a challenge as the previously known uniform representations by a Charles Lyall were attributed to a Charles James Lyall (1845-1920) who served as a civilian official in India. However, the absence of any biographic references to graphic works call into doubt his authorship of the "Armies of Waterloo".

Intensive Internet research led to the trail of another Charles Lyall who made his career as an opera singer. But the traceable, parallel career of this Lyall as a draftsman and cartoonist let us think, that he would more likely be the author of the plates. Ultimately, that became certain based on signatures both in well-known caricatures drawn by the opera singer Charles Lyall and in the published uniform plates. The "CL" can be clearly seen in the same format in both sets of works. So, the draftsman of the uniform plates must be the opera singer Charles Lyall.

The opera singer Charles Lyall was born in London in 1833 and died there on May 3rd, 1911. His lifespan corresponds to the 1894 publication of the series relating to the armies at Waterloo. A comprehensive biography of the singer can be found in the work "Victorian Vocalists" by Kurt Gänzl, published in 2017. Gänzl describes in depth his career as a (opera) singer, but also Charles Lyall's parallel passion for drawings and watercolours. Thus, first evidence of Lyall's drawing activity had been during a voyage of the to Australia, where he was identified in 1854 as "artist for black and white (printing) and watercolour works from Long Acre, London".

Back in England during the late 1850s, Charles Lyall began his career as a singer in several traveling ensembles. He performed tenor roles in Italian operas, mostly as a member of an ensemble at Covent Garden, London. Charles Lyall became one of the most respected performers in humorous roles in operas and operettas of his time.

Kurt Gänzl pointed out in his detailed description of Charles Lyall's singing career that he used his drawing talent throughout his life and also became popular for his caricatures of personalities of classic music - some of these cartoons were also published in the respected magazine Vanity Fair.

The plates of the "Armies of Waterloo" had been bound in four volumes. Due to his lack of military service, Charles Lyall either may have developed a love for colourful uniforms or just painted for customers. However, the existence of several sketchbooks, which are now in possession of the Anne S. K. Brown Military Collection, may point to the first reason, i.e., Lyall's interest in the - mainly British – military. Since Charles Lyall was not a contemporary of the Napoleonic armies, he had to refer to uniform plates published by other artists. References to them can be recognized, on the one hand, in the similar approach of the drawing style of his templates or, on the other hand, in the use of certain stances of the represented soldiers. The present volume about the Britsh army of 1815 is mainly based on the works of Hamilton-Smith from 1812-15 and Goddard and Booth from 1812. Perhaps Lyall also used uniform plates from contemporary artists such as Richard Knötel - although the year of publication, 1894, could speak against it, as most Knötel plates about the British army of 1815 were published afterwards.

Sketchbook of Charles Lyall
Anne S. K. Brown Military Collection, Brown University Library

Battle of Waterloo

After the 16 June 1815 battles at Quatre-Bras (see Volume 2 of this series) and Ligny (see Volume 3 of the series), Wellington had the unanswered question of how the Prussian army would move after their defeat during the night of June 17th. Would the Prussians move along their line of communication eastwards, away from Wellington's Anglo-Allied army, or still maintain contact to Wellington's army? The uncertain relationship between the British and Prussian leadership, that could be characterized as strong mutual distrust, was ultimately lessened by assurances from Blücher or his staff under Gneisenau that two Prussian army corps would arrive on Wellington's left wing on June 18th.

Wellington was therefore able to select a previously visited set of terrain on June 17th for a defensive deployment formation that had been proven in several battles Iberian Peninsula. He chose the field at Belle Alliance / Waterloo. Wellington recognized the potential of a slight elevation that crossed the street from Charleroi to Brussels, so that Napoleon could not directly see the reserves posted behind the crest. In addition, there were two key building complexes in front of the crest, which allowed trained soldiers to use flanking fire to weaken attacks on the Anglo-Allied line. One of these "obstacles" was the La Haye Sainte farm, which was centrally located east of the road to Brussels. The other lay in front of the right wing and consisted of the Hougoumont château located in a depression, protected by forested terrain that was difficult to traverse and had walled gardens offering further protection.

Wellington's plan was to arrange his troops along the top of the crest until June 18th, and to occupy the two strongpoints of Hougoumont and La Haye Sainte with reliable troops. Several brigades were to be placed in reserve behind the reverse slope, so they could be quickly brought up to appropriate front sectors in case of critical developments. Wellington's cavalry, which he did not value very much, was also located more to the rear; it also had the task of keeping in touch with the approaching Prussians.

Napoleon, on the other hand, believed on the basis of initial reports that the Prussian army had fled eastwards after the battle of Ligny, away from the now supposedly isolated Anglo-Allied army. He turned to Quatre-Bras on June 17th, where Ney's forces remained inactive since the battle of the day before. Napoleon feared Wellington could escape and therefore ordered cavalry to follow the retreating Anglo-Allied army. The allied rear-guard consisted primarily of British Light Cavalry, which was later assisted by Guards cavalry in minor cavalry skirmishes. An impression of these rather "symbolic" fights was provided by Private Playford of the 2nd Life Guards:

> „This day's work was more noise and sham than otherwise; each brigade retired in succession and the front had always a formidable appearance. The use of fire-arms on horseback had not attained much perfection. For on one occasion I watched the mounted skirmishers of the French and English armies, firing at each other for more than twenty minutes, and not one man or horse fell on either side."

The cavalry skirmishes were interrupted by a heavy rain, which soaked the entire ground so that horses could only proceed at a slow pace. The rain continued throughout the night of June 18th, so that the soldiers, who camped on the field after reaching their proposed positions, were drenched and hungry due to lack of supplies on the morning of the battle.

On 17th of June Napoleon was still convinced that Wellington would give decisive battle the following day and therefore the Emperor moved his army just a kilometre to the south of the Allied position along another ridge. Between the two armies lay lower ground, which the Napoleon's soldiers had to cross and then ascend a slight rise to engage the opposing forces.

Both army commanders deployed significant forces to protect against unpleasant surprises on the day of battle. Wellington feared his right flank could be outmanoeuvred and therefore ordered a British division of about 6,000 men and the Dutch-Belgian Corps of 10,500 men to Hal, about eleven kilometres away. Napoleon in turn ordered Marshal Grouchy with 35,000 men to follow the retreating Prussian army and to inform him about Blücher's activities as early as possible.

Thus, on Sunday, June 18th, 1815, the armies of Wellington with 67,000 men and Napoleon with 73,000 men faced each other across an area of about five square kilometres to fight the famous battle of Waterloo. Napoleon could rely on more artillery support because his 246 guns outnumbered Wellington's 157 guns.

The battle itself began at 11:30 in the morning according to many sources. After the French lost the battle they claimed the reason for the late beginning had been that the ground was the still wet, which would decrease the effectiveness of artillery. However, the incomplete deployment of the French units on the morning of 18th June is likely to be a further reason for the late start.

The map about the Battle of Waterloo published in this volume is from the rare atlas accompanying William Siborne's work "History of the Campaign of 1815." The other two maps of the Battle of Waterloo will follow in volume 4. These maps were selected because, among other factors, they show the situation of the terrain very clearly. The map in this volume shows the situation at the beginning of the battle with all the individual units and their commanders noted.

The Battle of Waterloo can be divided into the following four parts after the French artillery's cannonade opened the fierce fighting around 11:30:
1. Fighting around Hougoumont
2. Attack of the French army corps d'Erlon and counterattack by the British cavalry
3. Attack of the French cavalry
4. Attack of the French Guard infantry and the general attack the Allied army

At the same time as these engagements were occurring, the Prussian army made its appearance at Plancenoit on the right flank of the French army. Their entry into the fight tied up many of Napoleon's reserves that were ultimately missing for the decisive blow against Wellington's army.

Fighting Around Hougoumont

Napoleon's brother, Jérôme Bonaparte, was ordered to attack the château at Hougoumont with his brigade. Napoleon actually viewed this order as a diversionary attack, but during the actions the remainder of the day with efforts by Reille's entire army corps to attack, it could be that Napoleon planned more than a feint attack on Hougoumont

The infantry of the British Guards and Hanoverian and Nassau units positioned in Hougoumont's buildings and gardens were able to fend off the French forces' increasingly fierce attacks. The French succeeded at least twice in penetrating the Hougoumont château's courtyard, but each time the gate was closed again and all the expelled French – except for a captured drummer – were killed. A critical situation developed for the Anglo-Allied forces as they became short of ammunition in the afternoon, but it was remedied by the courageous act of a soldier of the Royal Waggon Train who rode to them on an ammunition wagon. Yet the French howitzers were able to set the roofs of Hougoumont's château and barn on fire with incendiary rounds.

Wellington recognized the danger now threatening the soldiers in Hougoumont and wrote an order with a pencil on a piece of cloth that today is located in the Apsley House in London:

> „I see that the fire has communicated from the hay stack to the roof of the chateau. You must, however, still keep your men in those parts to which the fire does not reach. Take care that no men are lost by the falling in of the roof, or floors. After they have fallen in, occupy the walls inside the garden; particularly if it should be possible for the enemy to pass through the embers in the inside of the house"

The approximately 3,000 British, Hanoverians and Nassau soldiers, with the support of another 3,000 men, a total of 13,000 soldiers were able to hold of Reille's French corps for the entire day so that they could not take Hougoumont. Thus the French forces were also not able to take action supporting the decisive e attacks on other locations on the battlefield. An example of the furore that prevailed in the fierce fighting around Hougoumont, was recorded by Richard MacLaurence, a soldier in the light company of the Coldstream Guards:

> „The emperor's commands 'Carry the post', while our Duke's were 'Keep it', and a most terrible post it was to keep. Once the French broke into the courtyard and such a scene of bayonet work, I, the narrator of this article never before or since beheld. It was fairly a trial of strength, the French Grenadiers were not to be trifled with and we looked like so many butchers, ret with gore, or rather like so many demons rioting against fire, for the shells had set two haystacks in a blaze and many a poor fellow lying bleeding and wounded, being unable to get out of the way, was burnt to death."

The French Corps d'Erlon's Attack and the British Cavalry's Counterattack

Around 13:30 more than sixty artillery pieces including sixteen howitzers were ordered to fire on the British front, above all to the east of the road to Brussels. In reaction, those forces positioned in front of the slope, namely the Dutch and Belgians of the Bijlandt Brigade were withdrawn to behind the hill. The soldiers of the units located there were advised to sit or lie on the ground so that the artillery projectiles would pass over their heads and not injure them.

The barrage was intended to prepare for the following attack by all four divisions of d'Erlon's army corps. About 14:00 it received the order to go into attack formations. Based on the bitter experiences with the firepower of the British infantry's line formation, they refrained from the normal formation of the typical attack columns. Instead the battalions were to deploy in line and form up behind one another in a compact "division column." The four columns formed in this manner were about 140-150 men wide and 24 men deep. The increased firepower achieved with this as opposed to the other narrower attack column was done at the expense of the more practiced employment of the typical attack formation. They would pay for this later when the soldiers in the division columns had significant difficulty in forming defensive formations against the attacking British cavalry.

After forming up, the four columns marched in chessboard-like arrangement, i.e., the left Quiot Division as the first, then the right Donzelot Division somewhat to its rear, the Marcognet Division again behind it to the right, and then outside on the far right the Durutte Division. The flanks of this attack formation were supposed to be protected on the left by the cuirassiers of the Dubois Brigade and on the left by the chasseurs and lancers of the Jacquinot Brigade. During their march of about 1,000 yards to the hill the four attack columns were taken under intense artillery fire and suffered their first casualties. While the left Quiot column was also fired upon by the Hanoverians and 95th Rifles in La Haye Sainte, the British Pack and Kempt Brigades received the two central columns with a broad salvo when it reached the crest. In the following bayonet charge by the British, the division commander, General Thomas Picton, was mortally wounded. Despite the, in part, heavy losses, the attacking French were able to take the crest-line and imagined themselves as victors, but then a loud shout of "Cavalry!" caused panic and the even the Durutte Division went to flight.

The cause for the shout was the attack by two British cavalry brigades, namely the so-called Household Brigade under Lord Edward Somerset with the Guards Cavalry to the west of the road to Brussels and the so-called Union Brigade under Sir William Ponsonby with the 1st (English), 2nd (Scottish) and 6th (Irish) Dragoon Regiments. These heavy cavalry units with about 2,500 horsemen were funnelled through the infantry units positioned in front of them and were not visible to the

French infantrymen until they were on the crest-line. While the Household Brigade, the "Blues," were kept in the second row in reserve, the Union Brigade's three dragoon regiments attacked as a whole.

The Dubois cuirassiers and especially many of the surprised infantry of d'Erlon's army corps were overrun by the attacking British cavalry. They were unsuccessful in forming proven defensive squares against the mounted attacks due to being in the unfamiliar division columns. They disintegrated from the rear and the French infantry fled towards their own lines. During this cavalry attack two eagles were also captured, namely that of the 45th French Line Regiment by Charles Ewart, Sergeant of the Scots Greys, and that of the 105th Line Regiment by Captain Clark and Corporal Stiles of the 1st Dragoon Regiment. The British infantry followed the attacking horsemen and thus captured another 2,000 or so Frenchmen and took them to the rear. Besides that, the fleeing French soldiers experienced the noise of rocket projectiles for the first time that were now being fired by the Horse Artillery under Captain Whinyates that had moved up to the crest.

Sergeant James Anton of the 42nd British Infantry Regiment tellingly described the events of this attack:

> „Horses' hooves sinking in men's breasts, breaking bones and pressing out their bowels. Riders' swords streaming in blood, waving over their heads and descending in deadly vengeance. Stroke follows stroke, like the turning of a flail in the hand of a dextrous thresher; the living stream gushes red from the ghastly wound, spouts in the victor's face, and stains him with brains and blood. There the piercing shrieks and dying groans; here the loud cheering of an exulting army, animating the slayers to deeds of signal vengeance upon a daring foe. Such is the music of the field!"

Only the Durutte Division and a few soldiers of the other three overrun divisions were able to form squares and retreat in good order.

But like had already happened in some battles in Spain, the cavalry who were confident of victory could not rein in their élan to attack and reached the forward French artillery that could not fire for a while in order to avoid hitting their own infantry comrades. In their élan the Union Brigade's dragoons did not hear the signal to withdraw and were themselves attacked in the flank and rear by the chasseurs and above all by the lancers of Jacquinot's brigade. With their exhausted horses the dragoons were defenceless against the lances and put up only weak resistance. In this French attack the commander of the Union Brigade, General Ponsonby, was also killed by a lance. The Household Brigade also fought with heavy losses, but primarily against cuirassiers. The surviving horsemen of both cavalry brigades withdrew to behind their own lines and had less than half their strength from the morning.

Thomas Hasker, a soldier of the 1st King's Dragoon Guards reported about the defencelessness against the French lancers and that by luck he survived:

> *„... in crossing a bad hollow piece of ground, my horse fell, and before I had well got upon my feet, another of the French Dragoons came up, and (sans ceremonie) began to cut at my head, knocked off my helmet, and inflicted several wounds on my head and face. Looking up at him, I saw him in the act of striking another blow at my head, and instantly held up my right hand to protect it, when he cut off my little finger and halfway through the rest. I then threw myself on the ground, with my face downward. One of the Lancers rode by, and stabbed me in the back with his lance. I then turned , and lay with my face upwards, and a foot soldier stabbed me with his sword as he walked by. Immediately after, another, with his firelock and bayonet, gave me terrible plunge, and while doing it with all his might, exclaimed, 'Sacre nom de Dieu!' No doubt that would have been the finishing stroke, had not the point of the bayonet caught one of the brass eyes of my coat; the coat being fastened with hooks and eyes, and prevented its entrance. There I lay, as comfortably as circumstances would allow, the balls of the British army falling around me, one of which dropped at my feet, and covered me with dirt; so that, what with blood, dirt, and one thing and another, I passed very well for a dead man."*

D'Erlon's defeated troops were able to rally for protection and form up again behind the artillery of Lobau's corps that had marched forward in the meantime. With the subsiding of the cavalry melee an hour plus pause ensued in this sector that was only interrupted by sporadic cannon and skirmishing fire.

The continuation of the description of the battle is in Volume 4 on the French Army.

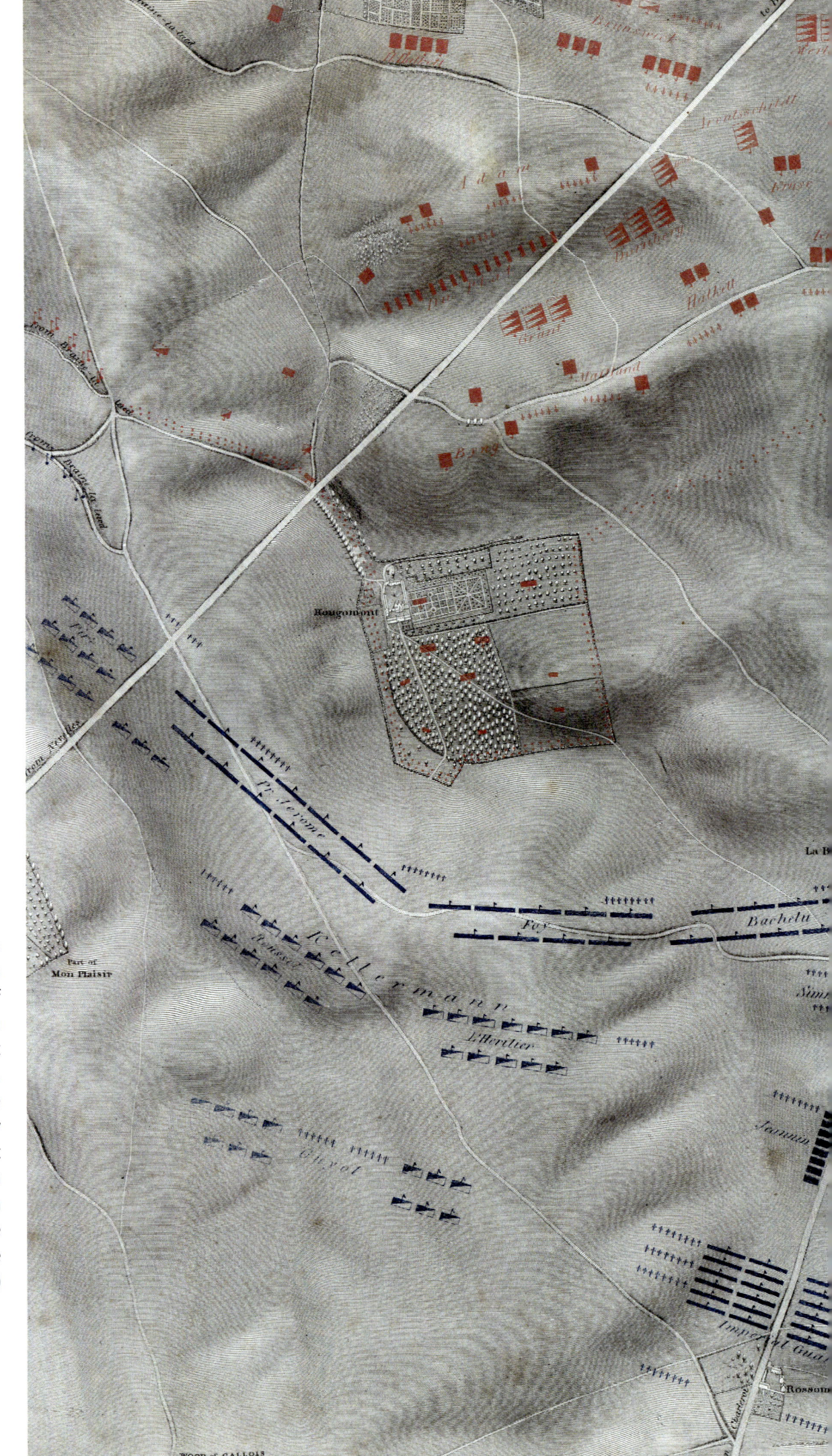

Positions of the Opposing Armies at the Battle of Waterloo on 18 June 1815 about 11:15 a.m. (Map from the atlas to the work by W. Siborne about the 1815 campaign that appeared in 1844; from the collection of the authors)

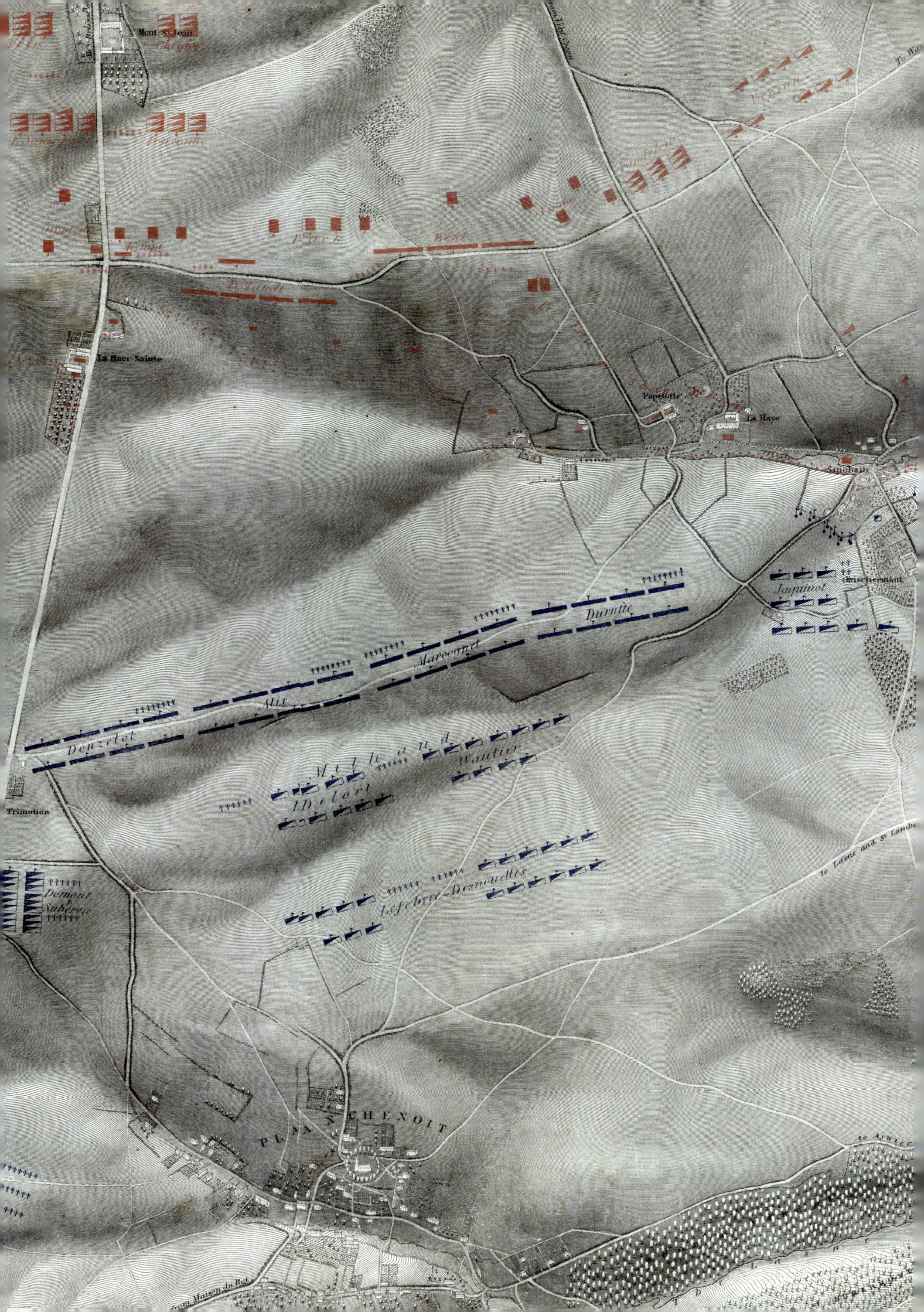

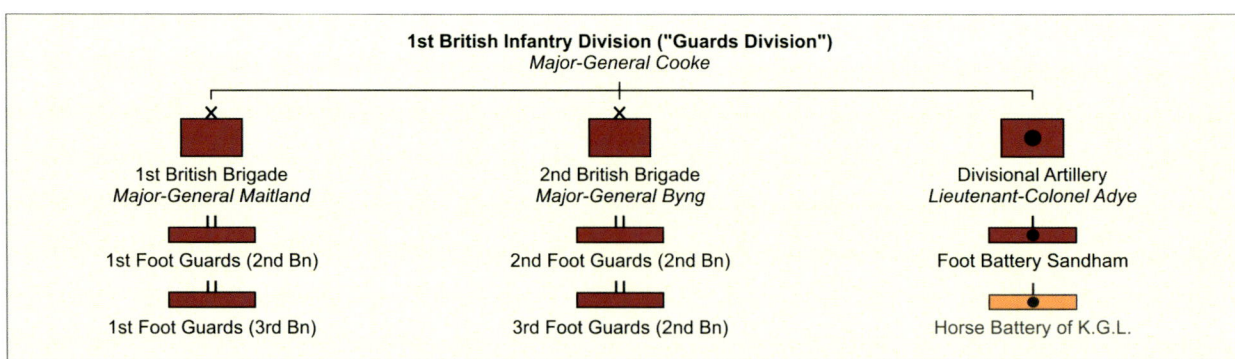
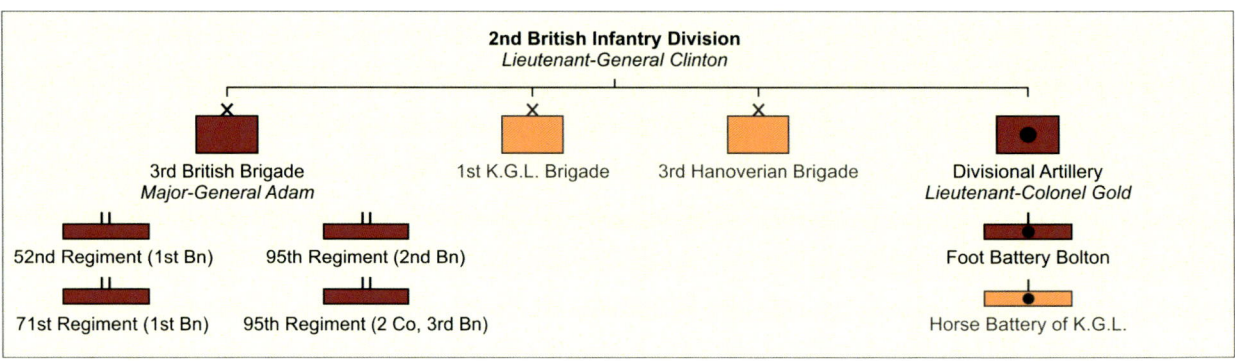
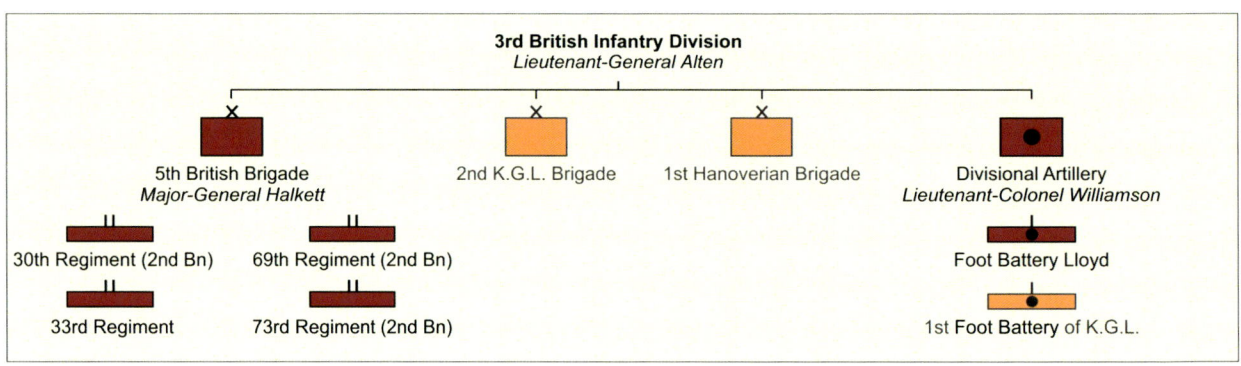
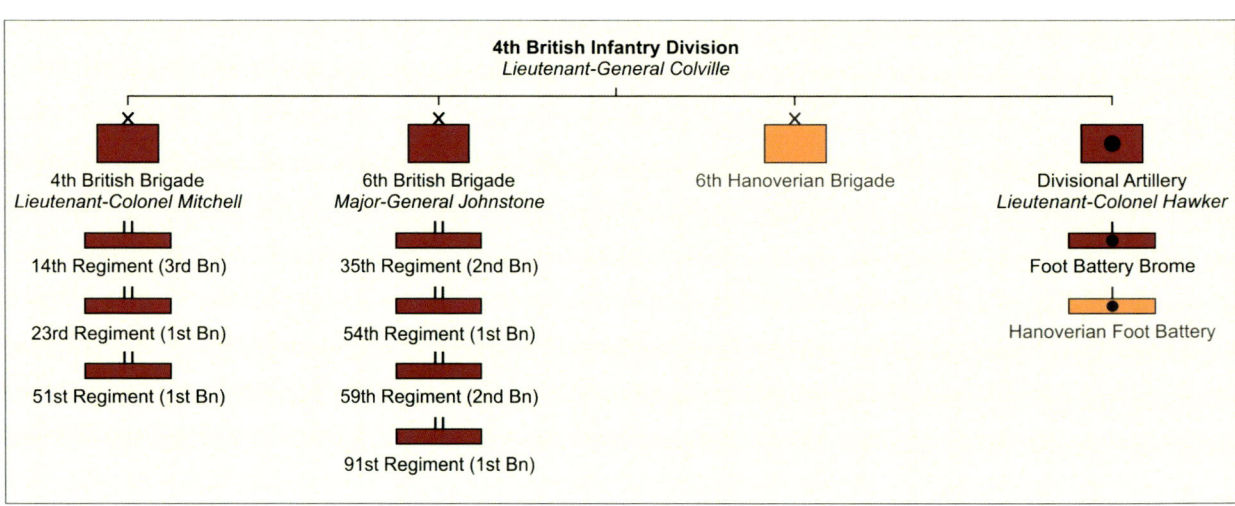

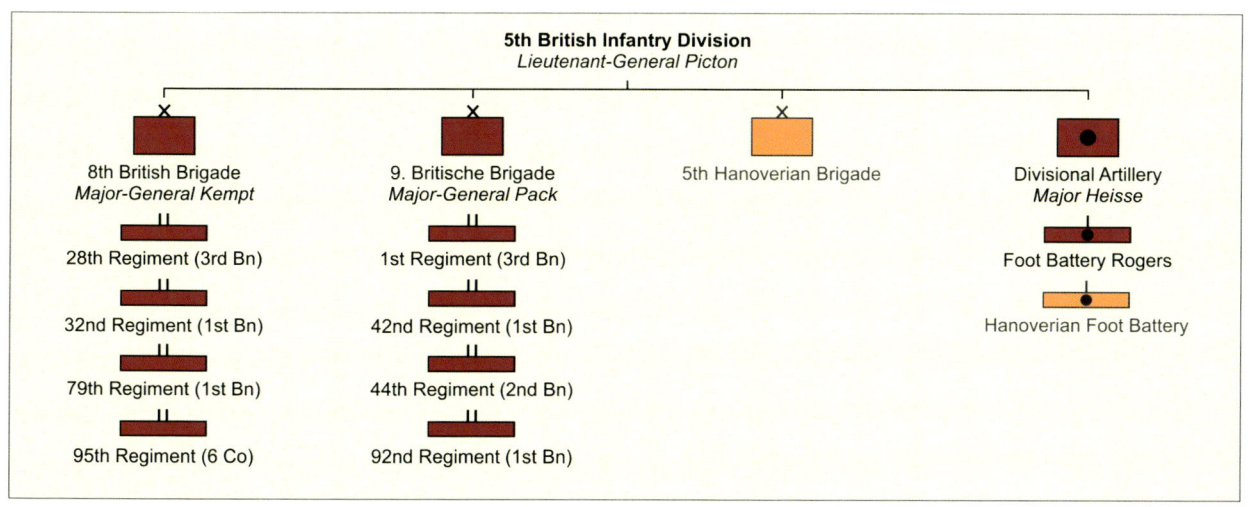
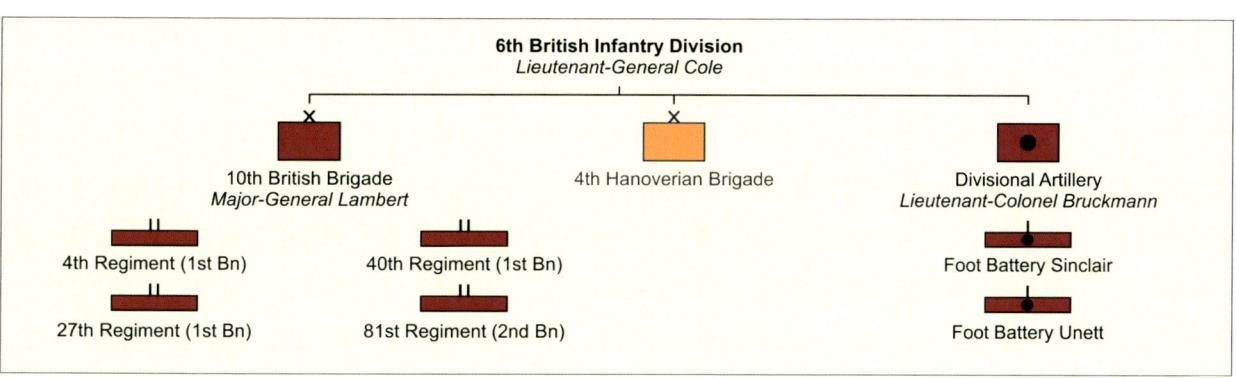

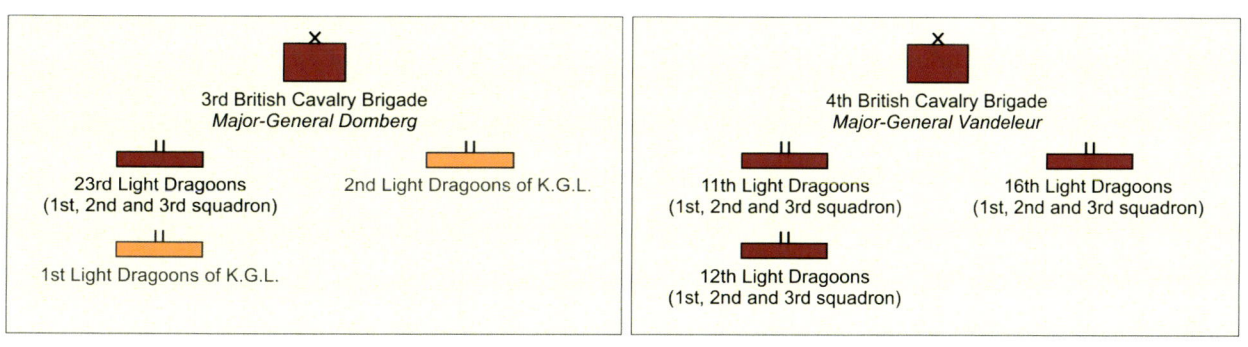

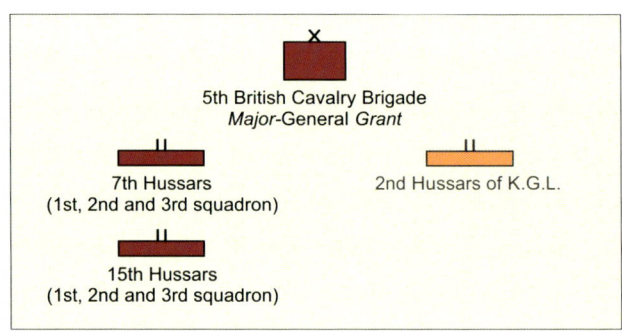
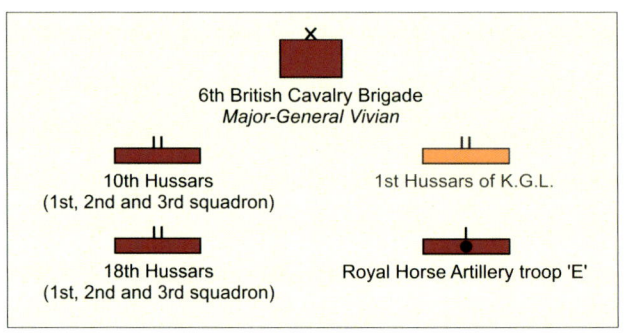
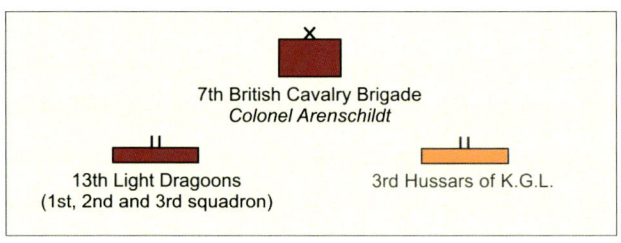
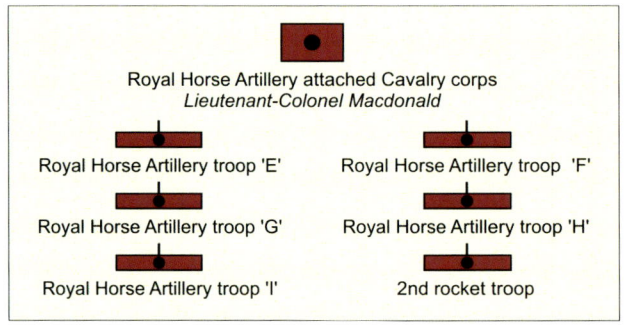
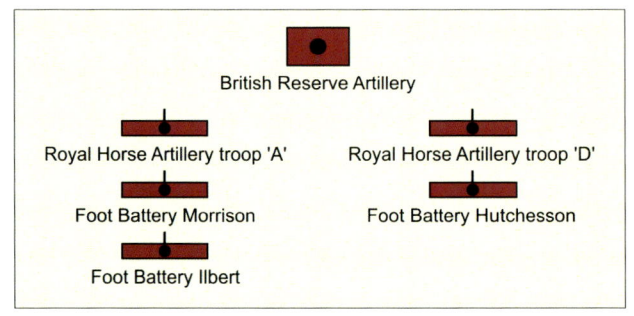

Organization and Uniforms of the British Army, 1815

Staff and Military Administration

1 – Organization

In comparison to the French Army, the General Staff was only authorized a few officers and divided across the brigade and division levels in the Quartermaster General's Department, that was responsible for the movements, quartering of troops and communication with the various commanders, as well as conveying orders to the forces. The next separate staff organization was the Adjutant General's Department, which existed as an organization at the army and at the division echelons. Its tasks were granting promotions in rank, issuing strength and casualty reports, as well as being responsible for discipline, drill and the intelligence service. The Provost Marshal was a separate staff that exercised military justice in large cantonments and carried out punishments.

As the senior commander, the Duke of Wellington's personal staff consisted of his military secretary and eight adjutants (Aides-de-camp). In addition, the Artillery and Engineer Commanders belonged to his staff. Wellington exercised complete control of the army and very often gave orders directly to the brigade or even battalion level bypassing other staffs.

In the British Army the following general officer ranks existed which were associated with a staff function or command of troops: The Field Marshal (at Waterloo only the Duke of Wellington), the Lieutenant-General and Major-General and finally the Brigadier-General. Additionally, the aides-de-camp, the assistant adjutant generals and the Quartermaster-Generals belonged to the staff functions.

2 – Uniforms, Equipment and Weapons

All senior and staff officers had a similar external appearance wearing a similarly cut red coat with dark blue distinctions and long coattails with white coattail turnbacks. The number and position of gold V-shaped embroidery on the front of the collar, on the facings, sleeves and on the coattails distinguished the officers' ranks. For example, a Lieutenant-General had nine embroideries in three groups of three on the facings; two sets of three on the sleeves and the same arrangement of the coattails. For a Major-General the arrangement was reduced to two sets of embroidery.

The Adjutant General or Quartermaster wore the same cut, however, with silver embroidery and the three sets of three embroideries on the facings and two sets of three on the sleeves. The aide-de-camp had no facings, but rather had a coat closed with a single row of buttons. The embroidery was S-shaped and was worn on the button stays on the breast, on the collar and on the cuffs.

In the field all officers wore a simple coat with less or no embroidery. The facings were often worn closed. They wore a simple bicorn hat and long pants in various shades of grey. On 18 June, a few officers – like Wellington or Picton – wore civilian clothing or that of their regiment like the Earl of Uxbridge, who was dressed in his uniform as the Colonel of his 7th Hussar Regiment.

Infantry

1 - Organization

The Infantry was the most important branch in the British Army of the Napoleonic Wars and the Duke of Wellington, who was somewhat sceptical about the use of cavalry, used the infantry as the fulcrum of his tactical formations. The British infantry's most important tactical unit was the battalion that included a total of ten companies. Battalions of the line regiments consisted of eight battalions-, one grenadier company and one light company, while the battalions of the light infantry exclusively received ten light companies. Often the line battalion's strength was cited as 1,000 men (so about 100 men per company), in any case the effective strength varied due to separations and casualties. The number of officers, non-commissioned officers and other cadre roughly corresponded to 10% of the total strength. The battalions of the three Guards Infantry regiments were nominally stronger with about 1,600 men.

In the 1815 campaign, almost all of the British infantry regiments only participated with a single battalion, and especially the regiments often only had two battalions and one of these was employed as a depot unit. Of the thirty-three infantry battalions stationed in the Netherlands in 1815, about half had been employed in the Iberian Peninsula theatre of war so they had experience in the fighting under the Duke of Wellington against the French.

The basic tactical formation of the British infantry battalion was the line. Actually, the regulations stipulated a formation in three ranks, however, the officers preferred a larger line in two ranks. The British infantry perfected the increased firepower on a broader front and effect was an instrument feared by the enemy troops.

2 – Uniforms, Equipment and Weapons

In 1815 a scarlet red coat, dark grey trousers worn over dark grey gaiters or boots (for the officers), as well as a shako characterized the British infantry's appearance. The shako for the line and Guards regiments was the so-called "Belgian" or "Waterloo" model and consisted of a felt body with a front plate. The latter was a brass - and for officers golden - sheet of metal on which, as a rule, was stamped the royal monogram "GR" and the regimental number. The cording was white for the battalions' companies and grenadier companies and could be green for the light companies; officers had cords of gold interwoven with crimson red. The small plume on the side was white over red for the battalions' companies, white for the grenadiers and green for the light companies. To protect against the rains which had already started in June of 1815, an oilcloth cover could be worn over the shako.

The light infantry (52nd and 54th Foot), the Rifle Regiment (95th Foot), as well as the 28th Regiment wore the old taller cylindrical shako without the front plate but with a hunting horn on the front. The Highland regiments (42nd, 79th and 92nd Foot) wore the characteristic bonnet with Scottish "Highland dicing" and black plumage.

Troops had a red single-breasted coat with an open collar, round cuff facings and short coattails. There was a white border along the edges of the collar and the shoulder straps. The buttons could be arranged evenly spaced, in pairs or in groups of three; additionally, white lacing could be added along the buttonholes depending on the regiment. The lacing could be varyingly shaped, namely simply square, with pointed ends or bastion-looped. The laces could have lines interwoven which were specific to the regiment. A further regimental distinction was made with the regimental colour visible on the collar, cuffs and shoulder straps. As a rule, the coattail turnbacks were white, and only the regiments with buff distinction colour had the coattail turnbacks in that colour. For the Guard regiments the cuffs also had a white edging.

Officers had more finely tailored coats with two rows of buttons, longer coattails and in some regiments with a silver or gold lace trim on the facings. These could be buttoned over so that the expensive trim was not visible when in the field or only visible at the top when folded over near the collar.

The following table lists the British regiments employed in the Netherlands in 1815 with the distinctions on their coats.

Regimental Distinctions 1815	Distinction Colour	White Lace Trim and spacing
First Regiment of Foot Guards	Blue	Pointed equal
Coldstream Regiment of Foot Guards	Blue	Pointed in pairs
3rd Foot Guards	Blue	Pointed in threes
1st Regiment of Foot (The Royal Scots)	Blue	Bastion-loop equal
4th or The King's Own Regiment	Blue	Bastion-loop equal
14th (Buckinghamshire) Regiment of Foot	Buff	Square in pairs
23rd (Royal Welch Fusiliers) Regiment of Foot	Blue	Bastion-loop equal
27th (Inniskilling) Regiment of Foot	Buff	Square equal
28th (North Gloucestershire) Regiment of Foot	Bright Yellow	Square in pairs
30th (Cambridgeshire) Regiment of Foot	Pale Yellow	Bastion-loop equal
32nd (The Cornwall) Regiment of Foot	White	Square equal
33rd (1st York, West Riding) Regiment of Foot	Red	Bastion-loops in pairs
35th (Sussex) Regiment of Foot	Orange	Square equal
40th (2nd Somersetshire) Regiment of Foot	Buff	Square in pairs
42nd (The Royal Highland) Regiment of Foot	Blue	Bastion-loop equal
44th (East Essex) Regiment of Foot	Yellow	Square equal
51st (2nd Yorkshire, West Riding Light Infantry) Regiment	Grass green	Pointed in pairs
52nd (Oxfordshire Light Infantry) Regiment	Buff	Square in pairs
54th (West Norfolk) Regiment of Foot	Green	Pointed in pairs
69th (South Lincolnshire) Regiment of Foot	Green	Square in pairs
71st (Highland) Light Infantry	Buff	Square equal
73rd Regiment of Foot	Dark green	Bastion-loop equal
79th Regiment of Foot or Cameron Highlanders	Dark green	Square in pairs
91st Regiment of Foot	Yellow	Square in pairs
92nd (Highland) Regiment of Foot	Yellow	Square in pairs

While the battalion companies' shoulder straps were attached to the sleeves with simple pieces of white wool, the grenadier and light companies wore so-called "wings" – these were red for the line and blue for the Guard and had regimental lace.

As a special distinction for the Highland regiments the troops wore kilts and the diced socks. Additionally, the 95th (Rifle) Regiment was issued its completely dark green uniform, with its coat having black distinctions.

Non-commissioned officers were distinguished by chevrons on their upper sleeves. Additionally, sergeants wore a crimson red waste sash worked with stripes in the regimental distinction colour; the Guard regiments sashes were only crimson red. Officers were distinguished by epaulettes with fringes of varying thickness, ornamentation on the epaulettes' face, as well as by a crimson sash. The sash was worn tied around the waist as for sergeants; only the Highland regiments wore it over the left shoulder.

The regular equipment consisted of a backpack covered with a black oilcloth, a black cartridge box and a bayonet. All of these were suspended by whited leather straps/bandoliers, but black for the 95th Regiment. A grey blanket was attached to the backpack. Additionally, there was also a water bottle and a bread bag.

As armament the infantryman in line and light regiments carried the Brown Bess musket; the rifleman in the 95th Regiment carried the rifled Baker flintlock. Officers were armed with a sword or sabre (light companies, riflemen).

For flags, as a rule each battalion had a pair consisting of the "King's colour" and the "regimental colour." The King's Colour was overall the Union Jack, while the regimental colour was distinguished by having its field in the regimental facing colour.

Cavalry

1 - Organisation

In 1815 this branch was organized in seven independent brigades (see Order of Battle). None of the formations was assigned to an infantry division, but rather their employment was determined based on the demands of the battle. The cavalry was divided between heavy regiments, formed by the dragoons and the Dragoons Guards (as the senior regiment) and the light regiments made up or the light dragoons and hussars. The Horse Guards was a special unit which with three regiments formed the sovereign's personal body guard.

According to the official regulations each regiment had four squadrons which each consisted of two troops. The squadron was the basic unit for movements in the field. In the 1815 campaign the number of squadrons and strengths varied significantly. The average complement at Waterloo lay at 477 men across all the ranks. Like for the infantry, the tactical formation was in two ranks divided into squadrons. The officers and NCOs were each positioned either in front of or behind the formation. It was typical for the light regiments to take on the reconnaissance and screening missions while the heavy cavalry was seen as the "attacking" and shock troops. In any case, time and again there was criticism of inadequate discipline during attacks or failures during ordered actions. Also, the Duke's opinion of the cavalry, based on his own experiences with that arm, especially in Spain, was not very high. During the Battle of Waterloo, the British cavalry showed it had the spirit to attack and élan, however it was not able to coordinate actions or to complete them successfully. This was clearly evident after the action against D'Erlon's corps when it was withdrawing to its own lines that the French cavalry could easily smash and cut down the scattered troops.

2 – Uniforms, Equipment and Weapons

LIFE GUARDS: They appeared very much like the heavy dragoons with a short red coat which had a yellow stripe (placket) along the breast seam. The collar patches were dark blue decorated with two yellow laces. The cuffs and the coattails were also dark blue. The belt had horizontal yellow-scarlet-yellow-scarlet yellow stripes. They wore long medium grey trousers with red piping/stripes on the outer seams. Starting in 1812 they wore a helmet imitating an antique model with a black bowl, brass coloured crest and a dark blue woollen caterpillar crest with a horizontal red stripe worked through it. A white plume with a red base completed the headgear. Equipment was a white shoulder bandolier with a cartridge box and a carbine strap. The weapon was a long, straight sword with a black leather sabretache with a brass star in the centre.

For field duty in 1815 the troops wore the frockcoat, a simply cut coat closed in front with a single row of buttons. The cloth shabraque was replaced with a white sheepskin shabraque with a medium blue edging and a grey cover.

The officers wore the same cut coat as the troopers, however, all the trim and lace were in gold. The trumpeters wore the uniform similar to the troopers except they had a red caterpillar crest on their helmets. A uniform variant has been shown with a yellow collar and broad shoulder pieces with a dark blue zigzag pattern.

HORSE GUARDS: in contrast to the other regiments, they wore a blue coat with red collar, cuffs and coattail turnbacks. Only the full-dress uniform had a yellow coat front seam (placket) with trim in the same colour as the facings. The waist belt was like that of the Life Guards. The trousers were also medium grey with red stripes along the outer seams. The helmet model was like that of the Life Guards with a black caterpillar and red central stripe. For field duty they also wore the simple coat with one row of buttons and the fleece shabraque and red trim stripes on the trousers. Officers and trumpeters were attired like for the Life Guards.

Regimental Designation 1815	Distinction Colour
1st Life Guards	Blue
2nd Life Guards	Blue
Royal Horse Guards (The Blues)	Red

HEAVY DRAGOONS OF THE LINE: For them the uniform looked like that described for the Guard. The Helmet however, had a horsehair tail instead of the caterpillar crest. The exception was the Scots Greys Regiment which wore a short bearskin cap with a brass plate and a visor.

In the field they wore long grey trousers with stripes on the seams. The trousers often had reinforcements of light brown leather on the inside and around the bottom. Armament was a straight sword in an iron scabbard. In addition, they were armed with the carbine. The shabraque was left behind on campaign, and a leather saddle with a grey blanket was used instead.

The trumpeters of the 2nd Regt. were dressed like the troopers. For the 6th Regt., trumpeters had red horsehair on the helmet and yellow swallows' nests with white trim.

Regimental Designation 1815	Distinction Colour	Other Distinctions
1st King's Dragoon Guards	Dark blue	Yellow front seam stripe (placket) with dark blue
Royal Dragoons (1st Dragoons)	Dark blue	Yellow placket
2nd Royal North British Dragoons (Scots Greys)	Dark blue	Yellow placket with dark blue
6th (Inniskilling) Dragoons	Yellow	White placket with blue

At Waterloo the DRAGOON GUARDS had only one regiment engaged, the 1st King's Regiment. Its uniform was no different than that of the heavy dragoons. The trumpeters wore coats with reversed colours, i.e., medium blue with red distinctions.

LIGHT CAVALRY: Although the Light Dragoons were dressed in the new uniform starting in 1812; the hussars received their own uniform on the European model after they were given that name.

The light dragoons wore a dark blue coat with short tails that was very similar to that of the French light infantry (*chasseurs*). Each regiment had its own distinction colour shown on the collar, lapels, cuffs and turnbacks. The waist belt was in the distinction colour and included two dark blue horizontal stripes. The epaulettes were in the button colour.

As headgear they wore a black felt shako that had a rosette on the front and had the upper shako band in the same colour as the buttons.

The pants for the gala uniform were white, however in the field, as a rule, they wore blue-grey, long coveralls that had seam stripes in the distinction colour and leather lining on the inside.

For the officers, like for the troopers, the button colours were respectively coloured, but in silver or gold. The leather cartridge belt bandolier was as a rule dyed in the regimental colour or red; variants were bordered in silver or gold. The officers of the 16th Regiment still wore the Dolman with cording from the period before 1812.

The trumpeter had a red shako plume but no cartridge box. For the 13th Regiment a buff collet with a red collar has been documented. Trousers with two yellow seam stripes. The uniforms of the other regiments' troopers had no further unique distinctions.

Regimental Designation 1815	Distinction Colour	Buttons
11th Light Dragoons	Buff	White
12th (The Prince of Wales's) Light Dragoons	Yellow	White
13th Light Dragoons	Buff	Yellow
16th or The Queen's Light Dragoons	Scarlet	White
23rd Light Dragoons	Crimson	White

HUSSARS: These formations all wore a dark blue dolman and pelisse with elaborate cording in the regimental button colour. The collar and cuffs were in the distinction colour. The troopers' pelisse had a black, light grey or brown fur edging according to the regiment. Long coveralls with light brown leather lining and cuffs and double seam stripes. The pants' colour varied from dark grey (10th Regiment) to light grey to light brown (also for the 10th Regiment).

Starting in 1808 the hussars wore the light brown busby with a short white plume with a red base, and cording in the regimental button colour. However, at Waterloo most of the regiments had replaced it with a shako covered with red cloth. In the front was a rosette in the button colour, as were the upper shako band and the cording.

In the field, the saddle blanket was also of sheep's fleece with a toothed cloth edge in the distinction colour.

The officers wore the same uniform, however, the cording and rank insignia on the dolman and pelisse were in the button colour. The cartridge box bandolier was usually richly decorated with gold or silver trim. The sabretache was red with the King's cypher.

The trumpeter in the 7th Regt. had a red collar, otherwise the trumpeters of the other regiments wore the troopers' uniform without and special distinctions.

Regimental Designation 1815	Distinction Colour	Cording	Headgear
7th Queen's Own Hussars	Blue	Yellow	Shako blue
10th The Prince of Wales's Own Royal Hussars	Red, 1815 Blue	Yellow	Shako red
15th The King's Hussars	Red	White	Busby & shako
18th The King's Irish Hussars	White	White	Busby (black)

ARMAMENT: The heavy dragoons and Horse Guards were equipped with the heavy cavalry's Model 1796 Model sword with a straight blade and scabbard of iron and the Model 1796 heavy cavalry carbine. The light regiments used the Model 1788 and Model 1796 cavalry sabres and employed the Paget Model 1808 carbine as the firearm.

Technical Troops

1 - Organisation

The artillery was administratively consolidated in the Royal Regiment of Artillery. Such varying units as the ten battalions of the (Foot) Artillery, the Royal Horse Artillery, the Royal Military Academy, the Invalid Battalion, Royal Artillery Drivers, the artillery of the foreign troops as well as the Field Train of Ordnance were united within the Regiment.

The foot artillery's tactical unit was a battery that was served by a company. This company included 116-124 artillerymen/gunners, 17 non-commissioned officers and 5 officers. The size of the crew depended on the battery's armament, namely whether more 6-pounder or 9-pounder cannon were employed. As a rule, a battery included five cannon and a (5.5-inch) howitzer. Attached to each battery was a troop from the Corps of Royal Artillery Drivers, with about 100 drivers. For a 9-pounder battery the train consisted of five cannons, a howitzer, a waggon with spare wheels, a fodder waggon, two baggage waggons, eight ammunition waggons and two supply waggons.

In the horse artillery so-called "Troops" served as the tactical unit and were designated with the letters "A" through "M" (except "J"). Each "Troop" consisted of 48 mounted artillerymen and 32-40 additional artillerymen who rode on the carriages of the five cannon and the howitzer. In contrast to the foot artillery, the drivers were integrated into the tactical unit and numbered 60 (for five 6-pounders and a howitzer) or 84 (for five 9-pounders and a howitzer). Furthermore, the Horse Artillery also included two rocket troops, of which one was always stationed in England and one was employed at Waterloo. In any case, Wellington distrusted the effectiveness of the "Congreve" type of rockets and therefore in May of 1815 ordered the "Troop" to be equipped with additional cannon.

The Corps of Engineers was divided into the Officer Corps, the "Royal Engineers" and the troops were the "Royal Sappers and Miners." Eleven officers of the "Royal Engineers" were assigned to the staff at the Battle of Waterloo, however, they were barely used due to the lack of requirements for their skills. The tactical unit of the "Royal Sappers and Miners" was the company that per regulations had within its ranks 30 carpenters, 38 masons and bricklayers, 10 smiths, 10 miners, 4 wheelwrights, 4 "collarmakers," 2 "coopers" and 2 painters. In 1815 ten of these companies were located in the Netherlands, of which two were on the scene at the beginning of the Battle of Waterloo. Within those two were also the Corps' Pontoon-Train.

Along with the artillery train there was also a supply train, the "Royal Waggon Train," which had sent a total of eight "troops" to the theatre in 1815. Of these, three probably took part in the Battle of Waterloo. The eight "troops" consisted of about 1,000 men and 1,440 horses that serviced the 100 ammunition and supply waggons, 27 fodder waggons and five mobile smithies.

2 – Uniforms, Equipment and Weapons

The foot artillery's uniform corresponded to that of the infantry but with reversed colours, i.e., a blue coat with red distinctions and yellow lace and trim. Depictions for 1815 show, in contrast to the infantry, red coattail turnbacks and no woollen tufts on the yellow-piped red shoulder straps. Also, the additional edging on the cuffs reminding of the 1st Foot Guards' cuffs is no longer recognizable. They wore the infantry shako with yellow cording for the troops as well as a white plume on the side. The brass coloured, or golden shako plate was similar to that of the infantry but with the inscription "ROYAL-REGT OF ARTILLERY" around the central "GR" monogram. Dark grey trousers. Whitened leather gear and cartridge box also of whitened leather. The cartridge box had a brass plate with a crowned shield on the lid. Equipment and weapons were like that of the line infantry. Officers had a blue coat with two rows of buttons, red distinctions and gold lacing. As with the infantry officers, they could also wear the (red) facings turned under so that the front appeared completely blue. Rank insignia were like that of the infantry.

The uniform of the horse artillery was oriented on that of the light cavalry. It consisted of a black "Tarleton" leather helmet with a black caterpillar crest and a white plume on the side, as well as the blue hussar style dolman with yellow cording. The dolman had a red collar and cuffs decorated with yellow lines. In the field, they wore dark grey overalls with leather reinforcement, and many illustrations show a red stripe along the outside seam. There is evidence of the M1796 light cavalry sabre being worn on a white belt – a suspension method also on the waist as well as of over the right shoulder. Officers had a similar uniform, only more elaborately decorated and with gold cording and braid, and a crimson sash as a rank insignia. In the field dark blue or dark grey trousers with leather reinforcement and red outside seam stripes were worn.

The drivers of the "Corps of Royal Artillery Drivers' wore a blue coat which is inconsistently depicted in representations from 1815-1816. It is either in the form of the artillery coat with red distinctions and yellow lace trim or simply with three rows of buttons which have yellow button loops. The headgear was a black "Tarleton" helmet. Grey pants with leather reinforcement and possibly with red seam stripes. Solders of the "Royal Sappers and Miners" wore the red infantry coat with a single row of buttons and blue distinctions and yellow lace trim on the collar, cuffs and in saw-toothed form at the brass buttons. Infantry shako with a white plume and yellow cording. The shako plate was rectangular with rounded corners. Grey pants, possibly with red seam stripes. Officers of the "Royal Engineers" wore the foot artillery coat with long coattails, though red with blue facings.

Soldiers of the "Royal Waggon Train" were dressed similar to the artillery train drivers but in red. The officer's uniform is not definitely established, although a red coat with silver hussar-like cording and six V-shaped braids on the forearms has been preserved. A bicorne hat and grey pants completed the uniform.

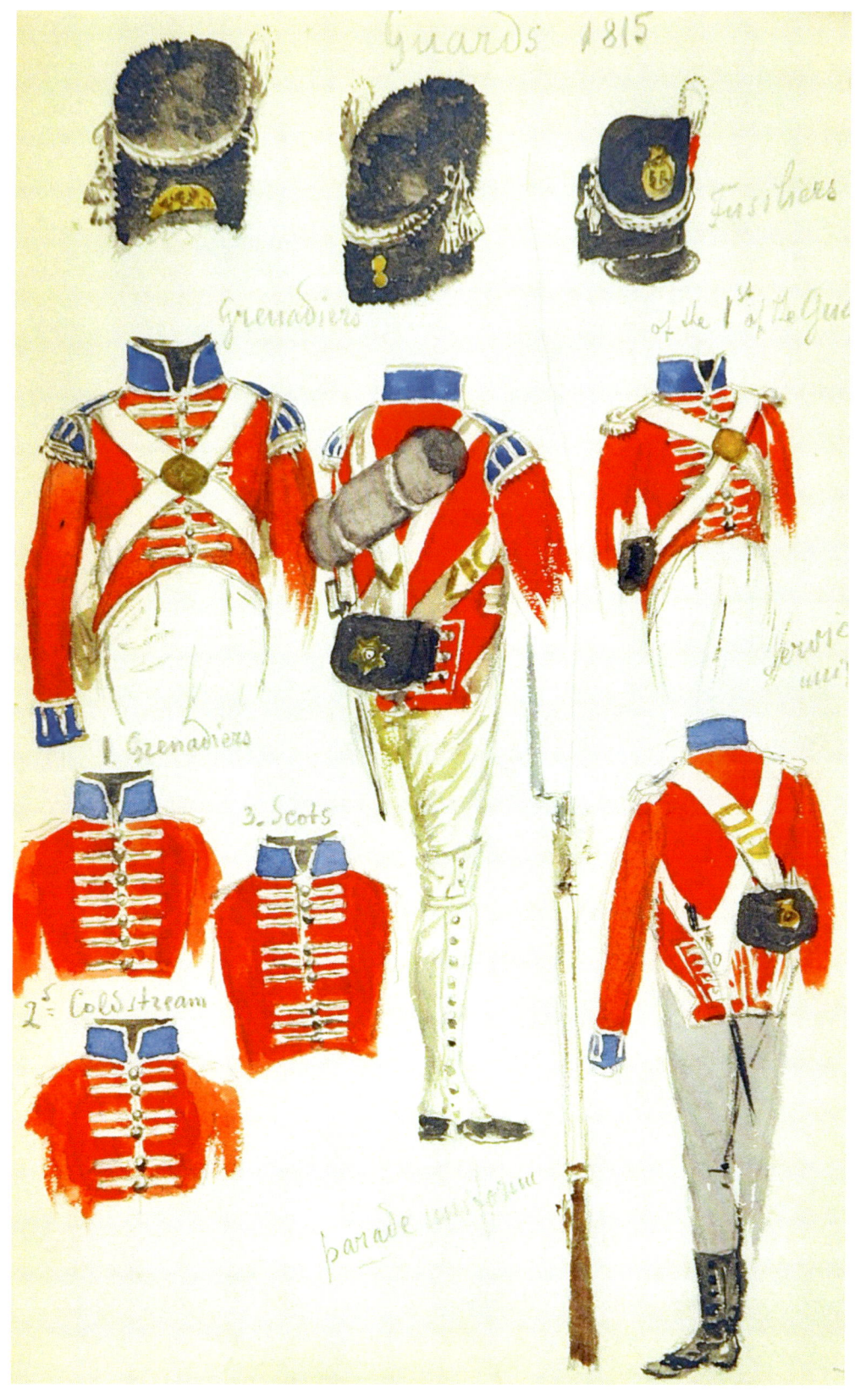

Sketchbook of James Lyall
Anne S. K. Brown Military Collection, Brown University Library

Texts below the pictures on the following pages were not in Lyall's original work but were added by the current authors.

UNIFORMS OF THE ARMIES AT WATERLOO

VOLUME 1
THE BRITISH ARMY

AS DRAWN BY
CHARLES LYALL
1894

Duke of Wellington
Commander-in-Chief of the Anglo-Allied Army in the Netherlands
The Duke, who chose the field around Mont-Saint-Jean/Waterloo for the decisive battle, was at the crossroads to Brussels during most of the battle. From there he was able to frequently move from one location on the battlefield to another to determine further actions. Eyewitness accounts tell that Wellington was forced several times to move to safe positions, even once into a square.
Uniform: The Duke was dressed in simple civilian attire. Over his coat he wore a black or dark blue cape. Whether this was decorated with loops, according to the sources, cannot be confirmed.
He rode a red fox (named Copenhagen).

Major-General of Infantry

The brigades of the British and Allied divisions/corps were commanded by Major-Generals, e.g. Major-General von Alten, commander of the Hanoverian units, or Major-General Maitland, who led a brigade which repelled the Middle Guard's regiments of Napoleon's army at the end of the battle.

Uniform: The epaulets are according to the regulations prior to 1811. The lapels were usually buttoned over when on campaign. The number and position of chevron laces show the rank. In service dress a pair of rather long, grey pants with or without trimmings were worn.
Source: after Goddard and Booth, 1812.

Lieutenant-General of Cavalry

The generals of cavalry led the brigades of the various cavalry units, e.g. the famous Union Brigade of Major-General Ponsonby, who counterattacked the French cavalry and died. Commander-in-Chief of the cavalry was Lieutenant-General Earl of Uxbridge, who was seriously wounded during the last moments of the battle.

Uniform: Typical were the high boots and the elongated, hanging plume.

Lieutenant-General of Cavalry

Uniform: As rank insignia the inverted V-shaped, gilded chevron, five of them for the Lieutenant-General. In addition to this, cords at the shoulder. In this illustration, the chevron lace would have to be visible on the coat tails. Many senior officers wore their own uniforms in the field, often consisting of a blue coat. Thus, the Earl of Uxbridge wore the hussar style outfit with the insignia of his rank. Source: after Ch. Hamilton Smith, 1812.

Major-General of (Light) Cavalry

This illustration is somewhat unusual as it contains elements of the Dragoons uniform as well as those of a staff officer. Although it was not uncommon for commanders to wear the uniform of their original regiment, the figure shown cannot be assigned to a possible historical person.

Uniform: Signs of the general rank are the lace pairs on the lapels. Clearly visible is the Mameluke style sabre, which had been popular among officers of all arms.

Source: after Ch. Hamilton Smith, 1812.

Major-General of Infantry
A general of this rank usually commanded a brigade or was assigned as staff officer. Thus, many officers of this rank who had served in the Spanish campaign had great experience in staff work. There was no General Staff employed in the British Army, as Wellington often issued his orders directly.
Uniform: On campaign the blue lapels were hidden. Four inverted V-shaped chevron lace and in pairs showed the grade.
Source: after Ch. Hamilton Smith, 1812..

Aide-de-Camp

These officers were personally assigned to the generals and had the dangerous tasks, e.g. carrying orders and dispatches to the different brigades/units. The senior Adjutants usually were at the rank of lieutenant-colonel or major. Wellington himself had eight of these important officers at his disposal. The losses at Waterloo were high, as six such officers were killed and twelve wounded.

Uniform: The parade uniform is shown, on campaign the service uniform without the laces was worn. Starting in 1814, a golden epaulette was worn on the right shoulder.
Source: after Ch. Hamilton Smith, 1812.

Staff Corps
This small unit was established in April 1810 but dissolved at the end of the Spanish campaign in 1814. It had the task of acting as dispatch riders for the staff and as military police and was responsible for capturing deserters. In the camp it had to ensure order. In August 1815, these special troops were re-established as part of the Allied occupation army in France.

Staff Corps

*Uniform: Starting in 1813, the Staff Corps was equipped in the style of the Light Dragoons. The buttons should be silver and the centre of the cockade black. For the saddlery, the cloak roll (valise) should be red with a blue border. As additional armament they carried a carbine.
Source: after Ch. Hamilton Smith, 1812..*

Officer of the General Staff

This part of the staff organization had the task of collecting and consolidating the unit strengths of various regiments and units and reporting these numbers. It also counted the losses and other statistics from various organizational levels. The officers were mostly assigned to the corps. The head of this corps, consisting of 21 officers in 1815, was Lieutenant-Colonel Sir E. Barnes.

Uniform: only one lace on the collar; the trouser stripes should be silver;
the rank was indicated by the number of laces, like for generals.

1st Regiment of Foot Guards, Soldier

The only Guard Regiment of the British Army in action with two battalions at Waterloo, which formed the 1st Brigade of the Guards Division. 1,628 men of the two battalions especially took part in the defence against of the evening attack of the French Guard infantry. They were later awarded with the title "Grenadier Guards" for this action.

Uniform: Field uniform of a soldier of the centre company ("Battalion company") with eight to nine rows of buttons (according to body height) equally spaced, with accompanying "bastion" rows of laces. Brass buckle and shako plate showed the embossed Star of the Order with "GR".

2ⁿᵈ Regiment of Foot Guards ("Coldstream Guards"), **Officer**
The 1,098-strong battalion of the 2nd British Foot Guards was united with the 3rd Foot Guards in the Brigade Byng and involved in the defence of the cháteau (manor house) of Hougoumont during the battle of Waterloo.
Uniform: Field uniform of an officer. The button rows should be arranged in pairs and the collar decorated with gold trim at the bottom. Epaulettes with thick fringes on both shoulders indicate a staff officer. The outer stripes of the grey pants are not confirmed.

2nd Regiment of Foot Guards ("Coldstream Guards"), **Soldier**

Uniform: The rear view of the field uniform of a soldier shown is based upon the presentation for 1812 by Ch. Hamilton Smith. However, the turnbacks should be white and provided with white edging. Skirt pockets with curved trim – four laces arranged in pairs. The cartridge box badge was prescribed for the 2nd Guards Regiment as a star - without a crown.

3rd Regiment of Foot Guards, Soldier

The second battalion of the 3rd (Scottish) Foot Guards Regiment joined with the battalion of the 2nd Foot Guards and participated in the defence of Hougoumont.

Uniform: Beautiful illustration of the dark grey woollen coat with two rows of six buttons; an attached cape should protect the shoulders. Shako cover of oilcloth with neck protection is indicated - but the shako plate probably could not be visible.

The knapsack and equipment are based on an image by Ch. Hamilton Smith.

Line Infantry, Sapper
*Uniform: Sappers after a plate by Ch. Hamilton Smith for 1815. An article by Reverend P. Sumner from 1943, identified the regiment based on the light green regimental distinctions and the simple white lace trim at the buttonholes as the 66th (Berkshire) Regiment of Foot - a unit that did not participate in the 1815 campaign. The cap plate shows a crossed saw and an axe.
Only sappers were allowed to have a beard.*

Line Infantry, Drum major

Uniform: This illustration is also based on the plate by Ch. Hamilton Smith for the year 1815, most likely for the 66th Regiment of Foot. The music band of British infantry regiments was usually splendidly uniformed, often in white, but also as shown here in "reverse colour design" – i.e., coat in regimental colour with red lapels, collar and cuffs. The attachment of the broad bandolier beneath the left epaulette and the silver lace shown by Hamilton Smith is incorrect. The drum major's baton should have silver decoration.

Line Infantry, Piper and Drummer

Uniform: These two musicians are also from the illustration by Ch. Hamilton Smith for the year 1815, like the sappers and the drum major. An army order of September 25th, 1811 mentions losses among the musicians due to their clearly distinguishable coats from those of the soldiers therefore prescribes coats in the same basic colour as the soldiers. A complete implementation of this order in all regiments is doubtful regarding the plate of Hamilton Smith.

23rd Regiment of Foot ("Royal Welch Fusileers"), **Soldier**
At Waterloo, 741 men of this regiment had been in the 4th British Brigade Mitchell and stood in reserve on the right side of the Anglo-Allied army and took part in the general attack on the retreating French troops – therefore, it suffered lower losses compared to other units.
Uniform: Representation based on a plate by Ch. Hamilton Smith for 1815. Distinguishing features of the fusiliers were the fur cap as well as "wings", otherwise provided just for flank companies of the Infantry. The expensive fur hat was to be reserved for parade purposes; in the field, therefore, the shako had been worn instead.

27th ("Inniskilling") Regiment of Foot, Soldier

The first battalion (750 men) was in the 10th British Brigade Lambert, which didn't fight at Quatre-Bras. It suffered heavy losses of up to 66 percent of the company in the centre of the Anglo-Allied army at Waterloo.

Uniform: Buff regimental colour also on the turnbacks. Lace should be rectangular and not as shown here with pointed shape. The knapsack should be covered with black oilcloth.

28th ("North Gloucestershire") Regiment of Foot, Colour Bearer

The 28th Regiment had 557 men in the 8th British Brigade Kempt and defended against the fierce attacks by the French corps d'Erlon at Waterloo.

Uniform: Buttons should be arranged in pairs, no laces, and the turnbacks are white. The golden tassels on the boots are not confirmed; however, the shako cords should have been golden. The yellow middle stripe of the sash is reserved for sergeants only. Hamilton Smith shows a colour bearer of the 9th Regiment with a carrying bandolier of whitened leather.

32nd ("Cornwall") Regiment of Foot, Colour Sergeant
The regiment suffered heavy losses of 266 men at Quatre-Bras. At Waterloo, the battalion was posted near the La Haye Sainte farm, left of the centre of the Anglo-Allied army.
Uniform: This depiction is also based on a plate by Ch. Hamilton Smith of the 9th Regiment with a colour bearer and guard (the task of the Colour Sergeant). Laces of the 32nd regiment should have been in pairs and rectangular. The middle stripe of the sash in regimental colour for sergeants is correctly shown.

33rd ("1st Yorkshire West Riding") Regiment of Foot, Soldiers

The second battalion of the 33rd Regiment had a strength of 576 men at Waterloo and was incorporated into the 5th British Brigade Halkett.

Uniform: Depiction of a part of square formation. The laces with saw-toothed "bastion" shape should be arranged in pairs. The absence a white piping on the cuffs is correctly shown.

42ⁿᵈ ("Royal Highland") Regiment of Foot ("Black Watch"), Soldier
Was assigned with 338 men to the 9th British Brigade Pack and fought at both Quatre-Bras and Waterloo. There it suffered losses in the centre of the Anglo-Allied army from heavy artillery fire and subsequent attack of the Corps d'Erlon.
Uniform: A soldier of an elite company after Ch. Hamilton Smith for 1812 showing the usual appearance of Highland regiments, namely cap, tartan and stockings. The coat as well as the blue-green pattern of the tartan are reproduced correctly. Starting in the 1790s, the regiment was allowed to wear a red plume on the cap; however, the yellow metal piece above the cockade is not confirmed.

44th ("East Essex") Regiment of Foot, Officer

During the campaign, the second battalion participated with the 9th British Brigade Pack.
It was located with 494 men at Waterloo in a central position and repelled
the attack of the Corps d'Erlon.

*Uniform: Similar to a plate by Ch. Hamilton Smith for 1812, a representation of an officer on duty,
as can be seen on the gorget being worn. Actually the 44th Regiment had silver buttons that should
also be sewn on the cloak. Not confirmed are the coloured coat lining (Hamilton Smith: white)
and the red stripe on the trousers.*

52nd ("Oxfordshire") **Regiment of Foot** ("Light Infantry"), **Officer**

The first battalion (1,130 men) was the strongest British infantry battalion during the 1815 campaign. It was located with the Brigade Adam on the right wing of the Anglo-Allied army at Waterloo and distinguished itself by its flank attack on the French Guards on the evening of the battle.
Uniform: Depiction after Ch. Hamilton Smith for 1814. Uniform of the Light Infantry; the turnbacks of the officer's coat in buff regimental colour are shown correctly. The cockade should be black with a regimental button and the coat buttons should be silver.

52ⁿᵈ ("Oxfordshire") Regiment of Foot ("Light Infantry"), Soldier
Uniform: Like the officer, this figure is based on the depiction by Ch. Hamilton Smith for 1814. Note the belt buckle with "52" in brass, while officers had the same in silver. Characteristic distinctions for the light infantry were the shako in its old form as well as the "wings" on the shoulders. The coat's lace should be arranged in pairs and the cockade actually should be black with white metal button.

69th ("South Lincolnshire") Regiment of Foot, Officer

The unit's second battalion (with 565 men) served in the 5th British Brigade Halkett. At Quatre-Bras it lost the regiment's royal colour. At the Battle of Waterloo, it was located in the centre of the Anglo-Allied army and defended in square against the attacks of the French cavalry for a long time.

Uniform: Depiction of an officer of the light company in parade dress – however the lace should be gold. Easily recognizable is the sabre, introduced in 1803 also for officers of the light companies, which, however, had a gilded handle.

71st ("Glasgow Highland") Regiment of Foot ("Light Infantry"), Soldier
Part of the 3rd British Brigade Adam, the battalion of the 71st Light Infantry Regiment was located with 936 men in a reserve position at Waterloo.
Uniform: First, the regimental colour of the 73rd Regiment is shown incorrectly. For the 71st Regiment, the flag should have been buff as well as the collar, shoulder pads, cuffs and turnbacks. The coat should have ten rectangular, white laces at regular intervals. The covered shako of the light infantry is correctly shown. Instead of the tartan trousers, dark grey trousers may have been worn at Waterloo.

73rd Regiment of Foot, Officer

The second battalion was in the 5th British Brigade Halkett with 498 men and had been positioned to the right of the centre of the Anglo-Allied army at Waterloo.

Uniform: Originally formed together with the second battalion of the 42nd Regiment ("Black Watch"), it lost the status of a Highland regiment in 1809. A staff officer of the centre company is shown here. A stripe in the centre of the sash in regimental colour was authorized for sergeants, only, so the drawing is incorrect in this detail.

79th Regiment of Foot ("Cameron Highlanders"), **Soldier**
The first battalion had a strength of 445 men and was assigned to the 8th British Brigade Kempt. After its combat at Quatre-Bras, the battalion suffered heavy casualties during the attacks by the d'Erlon's corps and from artillery fire.
Uniform: The plume as well as the missing sash, which was worn over the left shoulder, may identify the soldier as a private - however, this one should not wear "wings", but simple white woollen bulges on the shoulders. The coat's lace should have been rectangular and arranged in pairs. The stockings should have a red and white checked pattern.

92nd ("Highland") Regiment of Foot ("Gordon Highlanders"), Officer

The first battalion of the regiment had a strength of 412 men and was incorporated into the 9th British Brigade Pack. It fought at Quatre-Bras and in the centre of the Allied army at Waterloo.

Uniform: Silver laces, and not mistakenly gold as shown here. They should have been arranged in pairs on the (turned) lapels. The epaulettes should be silver. Officers did not wear the kilt in the field, but dark grey trousers. The method of wearing the sash over the left shoulder is shown well. A golden ornament over the cockade cannot be confirmed.

95ᵗʰ Regiment of Foot ("Rifles"), Officer
All three battalions of the 95th Rifles participated in the Waterloo campaign. While only the first battalion fought at Quatre-Bras with the 8th British Brigade Kempt, the companies of the 2nd and 3rd battalions fought in the 3rd British Brigade Adam at Waterloo.
Uniform: The uniform of this officer is confirmed in variants, except for the fur cap, by images from the Peninsular campaign - the pelisse with the dark brown fur, however, is described with white braids. A fur cap is not confirmed.

95th Regiment of Foot ("Rifles"), **Soldier**

Uniform: Except for the missing white piping on the turnbacks an accurate representation of the dark green coat and trousers. For 1813, Ch. Hamilton Smith also shows a soldier aiming his rifle, though kneeling. In the other illustration, the silver hunting horn on the shako is missing. The Baker rifle and the long bayonet sword used by the Rifles are reproduced well.

1st Regiment of Life Guards, Soldier

It was the oldest regiment in the British army. The regiment was united with its two squadrons (255 men) and the 2nd Life Guards as well as the Royal Horse Guards in the 1st British (Household) Brigade. When counterattacking the 1st Corps d'Erlon, the regiment reached the enemy's line before it was repulsed. The losses on this day were 18 killed and 43 wounded.

1st Regiment of Life Guards, Officer

Uniform: The field uniform with long, grey trousers is shown. Often, the single-breasted frock coat with buttons was also worn. The saddlecloth is part of the parade dress; on campaign simple grey blankets with sheepskins and simple equipment were used. The officer wore shoulder pieces consisting of twisted gold cords.

Royal Regiment of Horse Guards ("The Blues"), **Soldier**
Assigned to the 1st British Cavalry Brigade (Household) with two squadrons and a strength of 14 officers and 246 men. Positioned on the road to Brussels, it counterattacked French cuirassiers during early afternoon and successfully pushed the enemy back until the brigade went out of control and had to retreat with heavy losses (76 men).

Royal Regiment of Horse Guards ("The Blues"), **Soldier**
Uniform: The collar trim should also be at the top. The epaulets were actually red with yellow piping. The single-breasted skirt was used in daily service. No shoulder cords were worn on campaign. Here you can also see the parade saddlecloth, in the field, however, the grey saddle blanket with fur cover was used. Source: after Ch. Hamilton Smith, 1812.

Soldier of Heavy Dragoons
*Uniform: he wears the typical, long, red overcoat with cape over the shoulders. The white lining and the collar in regimental colour, dark blue for the royal regiments, is clearly shown. The coat was not worn during combat. The helmet was provided with a black wax cover.
Source: after Ch. Hamilton Smith, 1812.*

1st ("King's") Regiment of Dragoon Guards, Soldier

The only Guards Regiment of dragoons in the 1815 campaign. Not used on the Continent since 1794. In action with the Household Brigade, attacking the 1st Corps d'Erlon (against the 28th and 105th Line Regiments) during early afternoon and repulsing the French cavalry charge after the destruction of the Union Brigade. With three squadrons (588 men) it was the strongest cavalry regiment but suffered heavy casualties of 275 men during the fighting.

1st ("King's") Regiment of Dragoon Guards, Soldier
*Uniform: The yellow collar lace should have three dark blue, vertical stripes. The stripe on the trousers seam should be red. As a variant, a red collar flap is also shown on the collar's front side.
Source: after Ch. Hamilton Smith, 1812.*

1st ("Royal") Regiment of Dragoons, Officer

The regiment was part of the 2nd British Cavalry Brigade (Union) with three squadrons (455 men). On June 17, the Dragoons covered the retreat of the British Army towards Waterloo. During the following day, it attacked the advancing 1st Corps d'Erlon with the rest of the brigade and was able to capture the eagle of the 105th French Line Infantry Regiment in the melee. Heavy losses of 97 men were reported.

1st ("Royal") Regiment of Dragoons, Soldier

Uniform: The girdle should be yellow and blue, Gold and red was reserved for officers. The collar's lace should additionally have a dark blue seam. The pants should have two red stripes, Instead of just a blue one.

2ⁿᵈ ("Royal North British") Regiment of Dragoons ("Scots Greys"), Officer
Better known as the "Scots Greys" because of their grey horses. The regiment had seen no combat on the European continent since 1795. In 1815 it was united with the English (1st) and Irish (6th) Dragoons in the 2nd British Cavalry Brigade (Union) with the strength of three squadrons (444 men).

2ⁿᵈ ("Royal North British") Regiment of Dragoons ("Scots Greys"), Soldier
Their attack against the 1st French Corps d'Erlon led to the penetration of the enemy lines, advancing to the unsecured French artillery and briefly taking the batteries. Afterwards the regiment got out of control in hand-to-hand combat and was beaten back. However, during the fighting against French infantry, it was able to capture the eagle of the 45th Line Infantry Regiment.

2ⁿᵈ ("Royal North British") Regiment of Dragoons ("Scots Greys"), Soldier
Uniform: The sashes in the illustrations on pages 82 and 83 should be yellow-blue, and red-gold also reserved for officers. The epaulets of the dragoons are actually blue and yellow. The fur caps were often covered with black oilcloth in the field. The pants were strengthened with brown leather reinforcements on the inside of the legs. The sabretashe, made of black leather, was also worn in the field.

6th ("Inniskilling") Regiment of Dragoons, Soldier
This Irish regiment saw its first combat in the 1815 campaign and was part of the 2nd British Cavalry Brigade. It attacked the Corps d'Erlon with the remainder of the Union Brigade and pierced the French battle line.
Uniform: The collar's lace should have been white, for officers in silver. Yellow stripe on the pants. The sash also white and red. A sabretashe was worn.

Soldier of Light Cavalry
Uniform: Like the heavy cavalry, the light dragoons and hussars wore a long and bulky cloak during bad weather to protect their clothing and equipment. Here the colour was dark blue, and the collar was in the regimental colour. Officers' collars also had red piping. Generally, this garment was not worn in combat, but during the retreat to Waterloo some cavalry units may have worn this cloak.
Source: after Ch. Hamilton Smith, 1812

7th („Queen's Own") Regiment of (Light) Dragoons (Hussars), Soldier
Part of the 5th British Cavalry Brigade with 362 men, the regiment covered together with other units the retreat to Waterloo on the 17th June. The following day, the Hussars were involved in several defensive battles with attacking French infantry and cavalry.
The losses amounted to 202 men, 56 of them killed.

7th ("Queen's Own") Regiment of (Light) Dragoons (Hussars), Soldier
Uniform: The plate by Hamilton Smith shows a hussar ca. 1813 very well. From 1814 onwards, the uniform colour should be dark blue with yellow laces. The shako slowly replaced the unpopular fur hat. The pants were also dark blue and had yellow stripes. On the left side was a saber strap with a black leather sabretashe.

10th ("Prince of Wales's Own Royal") Regiment of (Light) Dragoons (Hussars), Soldier
The regiment was used in a rear-guard action against attacking French cavalry during the day of 17 June. On 18 June, it was part of the 6th Cavalry Brigade Vivian with 452 men and was positioned on the left wing, and together with the 18th Hussars covered the flank from enemy attacks, e.g., by the French Division Durutte towards the farm of Papelotte.

10th ("Prince of Wales's Own Royal") **Regiment of** (Light) **Dragoon**s (Hussars)**, Officer**
Uniform: The Hussar corresponds to the plate by Hamilton Smith with red facings and white laces worn until 1814. Afterwards these changed to blue with yellow laces, for officers golden. Shakos were also introduced. The stripe on the pants seam should be red.

11th Regiment of (Light) Dragoons, Officer
Also positioned on the left wing of the English front, the regiment (442 men) was part of the
4th Cavalry Brigade Vandeleur and deployed during the early afternoon to relieve the scattered
Union Brigade, pushing back cuirassiers and lancers.
*Uniform: The buttons should be white; the stripes on the trousers seam silver.
The stripes of the officers' sash were always gold and red.*

12th ("Prince of Wales's") Regiment of (Light) Dragoons, Officer
This regiment was part of the 4th Cavalry Brigade Vandeleur together with the 11th Light Dragoons and took part in several attacks to relieve the severely battered Union Brigade and protected their remnants. The 12th Light Dragoons recorded a loss of 46 killed and 60 wounded.
Uniform: Buttons in silver; the missing cartridge bandolier should be edged in yellow and silver.

13th Regiment of (Light) Dragoons, Soldier
After operations in the rear-guard fighting on June 17th, on the next day the regiment was positioned on the right wing behind Hougoumont. It was assigned to the 5th Cavalry Brigade Grant with 455 men. During the course of the battle, the brigade repeatedly pushed back the French cuirassier attacks against the British squares. In the evening, it took part in the general pursuit of the retreating French army.

13th Regiment of (Light) Dragoons, Soldier

Uniform: The facing colour should be lighter, according to a regimental listing rather it should be buff. No white trim on the cuffs. The trouser stripes are in facing colour. The epaulettes like the buttons in yellow. In field shako covers were worn often, as further equipment they used the light blue water bottle as well as a linen bag for the personal things.

15th ("King's") Regiment of (Light) Dragoons (Hussars), Soldier
Although in position behind Hougoumont with the 5th Cavalry Brigade Grant, the unit participated in no major operations on the day of the battle. However, they suffered considerable losses from enemy artillery fire, including 22 killed.

15th ("King's") Regiment of (Light) Dragoons (Hussars), Soldier
Uniform: The plate by Ch. Hamilton Smith shows the typical hussar uniform in 1815, except for the missing laces at the collar, the sabretashe and the red stripes on the trousers. In 1815, the regiment had also mostly adopted red-covered shakos.
The officers wore silver cording and trouser seam stripes.

16th ("Queen's Own") Regiment of (Light) Dragoons, Officer
Initially positioned on the left wing, the regiment supported the attack of the Union Brigade during the early afternoon of June 18, pushed through a French battery and continued to repulse an advancing French Chevaulegers regiment. In the later course of the major French cavalry attacks, the Dragoons counterattacked charging cuirassiers near Ohain.
Uniform: Buttons and side stripes should be silver, and the bandolier should have a heart-shaped badge.

18th ("King's Irish") Regiment of (Light) Dragoons (Hussars), Soldier
Until the afternoon of the 18th June, the regiment stood on the far-left wing with the 6th Cavalry Brigade Vivian. During the French cavalry attacks on the British lines, the brigade commander personally led the hussars against advancing French chasseurs á cheval and horse grenadiers of the Imperial Guard. During the attack it rode through a battery of French horse artillery that it destroyed. The French Guard's regiments threw the hussars back to their own lines.
The regiment's casualties of June 18th included 13 killed and 74 wounded.

18th ("King's Irish") Regiment of (Light) Dragoons (Hussars), Soldier
Uniform: The plate by Hamilton Smith corresponds to the uniform for 1815; officers wore similar uniforms with silver lacing and trim. The pants stripes should be red and the lacing on pelisse and dolman smaller and with loop decorations. The regiment also wore dark blue trousers in 1815.

23rd Regiment of (Light) Dragoons, Officer
This regiment was assigned to the light cavalry of the King's German Legion in the 3rd Cavalry Brigade Dörnberg. It was located on the right wing behind Hougoumont and counterattacked French cavalry during the afternoon.
Uniform: Because the buttons were golden, the upper shako trim should have been in the same colour - for soldiers yellow - as well as the epaulettes.

Royal Regiment of Artillery, Soldier of Foot Battery
A total of 13 batteries of the regiment took part in the campaign of 1815, including eight of the mounted artillery - one of them equipped with rockets. The batteries contained a total of 78 guns that fired about 10,400 rounds during the Battle of Waterloo. Losses among soldiers and officers were low compared to the other branches.
Uniform: Based on a plate by Ch. Hamilton Smith from 1815. During campaigns, dark grey trousers were worn. The regular artillery saber had a more angular grip.

Royal Regiment of Artillery, Soldier of Foot Battery

Uniform: Depiction after a plate by Ch. Hamilton Smith from 1815. It shows two gunners near a typical garrison gun, probably in service in England. Dark grey pants were worn in field service. The white cartridge pouch is a special feature of the British artillery, however, the red cloth beneath the emblem is shown only in a few contemporary images. Some images also show white turn-backs. Confusing portrayal of the bandoliers, as the saber bandolier should run from the right shoulder below the cartridge pouch bandolier. Also, the collar was round in the back and not pointed like on this depiction.

Royal Regiment of Artillery, Officer of the "Royal Horse Artillery"
Uniform: The plate corresponds to the order of the Prince Regent, given on January 14, 1812 - where he directed the laced jacket with white breeches and black boots with gold trim as parade dress. The plume should be white. The jacket actually has significantly more rows of buttons and laces (an existing original has 23). The collar should also have yellow edgings. As rank insignia a sash and (not regular) sleeve insignia are shown. The black waist belt is known for the evening service dress.

Royal Regiment of Artillery, Gunner or Officer of the "Royal Horse Artillery"
Uniform: Only the horse equipment is shown correctly. The uniform is faulty in several parts, namely a "Tarleton" helmet with neck protection, a closed collar without the yellow lace and a small number of braids. The sash was reserved to officers or staff officers only. The pants are documented in this form; the black waist belt is confirmed only for officers. The Rocket Corps generally carried cartridge pouches on a shoulder bandolier.

Royal Regiment of Artillery, Soldier of the Rocket Troop

A troop of the Royal Horse Artillery was equipped with rockets of the Congreve type. The troop was used during the Battle of Waterloo on the left wing of the Allied army. It launched 52 rockets in support of the Ponsonby cavalry charge.

Uniform: Depicted on a plate by Ch. Hamilton Smith of 1815. The uniform in based on that of the Light Cavalry. Each soldier was mounted and was supposed to carry three to four rocket poles.

Royal Regiment of Artillery, Soldier of the Rocket Troop

Uniform: Exact copy of the plate by Ch. Hamilton Smith done in 1815. However, the jacket of the (mounted) artillery was darker and it had more rows of buttons and laces - see also the faulty representation of the mounted artillery. The closed collar is certainly wrong, as it was open for the whole English army.
The red lining of the crowns on the saddlecloth is also shown by Hamilton Smith..

Royal Regiment of Artillery, Driver of the "Royal Horse Artillery"
In contrast to the foot artillery, the mounted artillery had drivers in their rank and file, which comprised about one third of the field strength of a battery.
Uniform: Based upon a plate by Ch. Hamilton Smith for 1815. However, Hamilton Smith shows the cuffs and the collar with a narrow yellow edging, but not the yellow lace on the collar. The button rows each are framed by a narrow yellow piping, in addition there is piping along the entire lapels. The red chevron on the upper arm is also shown by Hamilton Smith.

Royal Sappers and Miners, Soldier

Created in 1813 from the Royal Military Artificers and Laborers, ten companies (including two as pontoon train) of the Royal Sappers and Miners were stationed in the Netherlands in 1815 - but they did not participate in the Battle of Waterloo.

Uniform: Based on a plate by Ch. Hamilton Smith for 1815. The red outer stripe on the trousers is not shown there but is confirmed for the simple red jacket of the working uniform. Also, the shako badge does not correspond to the "infantry pattern" shown here, but had been a trapezoidal, large brass shield with embossing. Epaulettes were only edged along the outside and the buttonholes with yellow piping. The collar also had piping along the lower edge.

Royal Engineers, Officer
The corps of the Royal Engineers consisted exclusively of officers and counted a total of 263 Engineers throughout the English Army in 1815. Of the 61 identifiable Engineers in the Netherlands, only eleven participated in the Battle of Waterloo.
Uniform: Depiction after Ch. Hamilton Smith of 1815. The red coat with blue facings (slightly lighter than the dark blue of the Foot Guards) and golden laces should replace the former dark blue uniform from 1812 onwards. The uniform shown here may have been worn at Waterloo.

Royal Waggon Train, Soldier
Eight British "Troops" with about 1,000 men were responsible for the transport of supplies (including ammunition) in the Netherlands during the campaign. Three troops were probably used at Waterloo. The personal actions of driver Brewer, who supplied the troops of Hougoumont with much needed ammunition during the afternoon, became famous.
Uniform: Based on a plate by Ch. Hamilton Smith for 1812. There, however, grey trousers and black gaiters are shown. For the jacket and headgear, see the comments regarding the following plates..

Royal Waggon Train, Driver

Uniform: The headgear displayed on the three plates of the Royal Waggon Train soldiers resembles a fur hat. Hamilton Smith, however, shows a simple shako with a small red and white plume and a black cockade with a pewter button on the front - the cords should be white. The blue pants and the heavy riding in the version shown here by Hamilton Smith have been confirmed.

Royal Waggon Train, Driver

Uniform: Hamilton Smith shows the soldier's coat with pointed cuffs on all three plates. The white lace can be found along all edges of the collar - not just like here in front and top - and in kind of a border around the button rows. The piping along the edge of the coat and the buttonholes were narrower than shown here - the pattern was in the same manner as for the riders of the artillery train.

Royal Waggon Train, Officer

Uniform: The plate by Ch. Hamilton Smith also shows the rear view of a mounted officer with a cocked hat. However, no white edging on the collar and no silver lace on the pants is shown there. A preserved original coat confirms the six V-shaped laces on the turn-backs. Hamilton Smith shows the mounts for the cloak bag in black. The M 1796 light cavalry saber shown had a white metal handle.

Royal Waggon Train, Officer

Uniform: The coat depicted here is confirmed neither by Hamilton Smith nor by a known preserved officer's uniform. The existing coat has silver braids in the style of Hussar jackets and six silver V-laces on the forearms. No white edging of collar and cuffs. In addition to the cocked hat, which was used in the field, the officers also wore the helmet M 1812 of the Light Dragoons with silver lacing.

Annotated Selected Bibliography

The following are recommended as introductory and more detailed literature on the 1815 campaign and on the uniforms and equipment of the British Army of 1815. This list focuses primarily on the literature that is still more readily available.

1 – Literature on the 1815 Campaign

The following recommended works about the 1815 campaign are among the newer literature and provide information on the campaign from various viewpoints:

1. Adkin, Mark, The Waterloo Companion (London: Stackpole Books, 2001). *Excellent, comprehensive work with that looks as all aspects of the campaign.*
2. Buttery, David, Waterloo Battlefield Guide (Barnsley: Pen and Sword, 2013). *Among the numerous guides to the 1815 campign battlefields, it is one of the most comprehensive and up-to-date.*
3. 3. Coppens, Bernard, Les mensonges de Waterloo (Brussels: Jourdan, 2009). *This expert on the 1815 campaign gives new evaluations of controversial aspects using current sources.*
4. Courcelle, Patrice et al., Les Carnets de la Campagne (Montrouge, 1999-2015): La Belle Alliance). Currently 15 issues published have been since 1999. *These illuminate various actions of the campaign in detail, especially the Battle of Waterloo, each also supplemented with a chapter on uniforms.*
5. Field, Andrew, Waterloo – The French Perspective (Barnsley: Pen and Sword, 2012). *One of the few modern presentations giving the French perspective.*
6. Franklin, John, Waterloo 1815 (three issues from the Osprey Campaign series, Oxford: Osprey, 2015). *Introduction to the three battles of the 1815 campaign by an author with knowledge of numerous eyewitness reports.*
7. Glover, Gareth, Waterloo – The Defeat of Napoleon's Imperial Guard (Barnsley: Pen and Sword, 2015). *A very well researched work on the final turning point of the Battle of Waterloo.*
8. Glover, Gareth, The Waterloo Archive (Barnsley: Pen and Sword, 2010–2014), six volumes. *A collection of numerous contemporary British and German reports and memoirs.*
9. Glover, Gareth, Waterloo, Myth and Reality (Barnsley: Pen and Sword, 2014). *A current work on the Battle of Waterloo that considers numerous reports by participants of the battle.*
10. Hofschroer, Peter, 1815 – The Waterloo Campaign – the German Victory. (London: Greenhill, 1998–1999, two volumes). *Despite the author being controversial, this is an important work specially focused on the role of German forces in the 1815 campaign.*
11. Muilwijk, Erwin, The Netherland's Field Army during the Waterloo Campaign (Bleiswijk: Sovereign House, 2014). *Currently three volumes about the 1815 campaign with an extensive look at the Dutch-Belgian units.*

Along with many other works providing a deeper understanding, two classics are particularly recommended, namely William Sibornes "Waterloo Campaign 1815," that was initially published in 1844 and is an important work based on the methodical interviews of participants of the campaign. The British side is complemented by the French work by Henry Houssaye "1815 Waterloo," that first appeared in 1893. Both works are available in a digital or printed reproduction form. For further literature and sources see the portal on the 1815 campaign at (http://feldzug1815.de/index.php/arbeitsmittel/1-literatur).

2 – Literature on the British Army

1. Fosten, Bryan, Wellington's Infantry (1), Wellington's Infantry (2), Wellington's Heavy Cavalry and Wellington's Light Cavalry. (London: Osprey, 1981-1982). *Multiple volumes in the Men-at-Arms series about the organization and uniforms. A solid introduction to and overview of the topic with informative plates also prepared by Bryan Fosten.*
2. Fletcher, Ian, Napoleonic Wars – Wellington's Army (London: Brassey's 1996). *A general and good treatment of Wellington's armies with regard to the British army in 1815.*
3. Fletcher, Ian, Wellington's Foot Guards (Elite series No. 52) (London: Osprey, 1994). *Looks at the history and uniforms of the Foot Guards from 1798 until after Waterloo.*
4. Franklin, C. E., British Napoleonic Uniforms (Stroud: The History Press, 2008). *Comprehensive presentation on the uniforms from 1798 to 1815 in the form of computer-generated colour plate with commentaries.*
5. Haythornthwaite, Philip J., Wellington's Specialist Troops, (Men-at-Arms No. 204), London: Osprey, 1988).
6. Haythornthwaite, Philip J., British Infantry of the Napoleonic Wars (London: Arms and Armour, 1987).
7. Haythornthwaite, Philip J., Uniforms of Waterloo (London: Blandford Press, 1974). *A classic among the newer studies of the Waterloo armies. Very well illustrated and has thorough descriptions of the uniforms and history of the branches and units.*
8. Haythornthwaite, Philip J., Wellington's Army - The Uniforms of the British Soldier,1812–1815 (London: Greenhill, 2002). *Very well annotated, large format edition of Charles Hamilton Smith's series of uniform plates.*
9. Lawson, Cecil C. P., A History of the Uniforms of the British Army, Volume V. (London: Norman Military Publications, 1967). *The standard work on uniforms and source studies about the British Army.*
10. Mollo, John, Waterloo Uniforms, British Cavalry (London: Historical Research Unit, 1973). *In depth study about the British cavalry with very many contemporary illustrations and descriptions.*
11. Nafziger, G. F./Park, S. J., The British Military System and Organization 1803–1815 (Cambridge: Rafm Co., 1983). *A very good overview of the structure and organization of the army.*
12. North, Rene, Regiments at Waterloo (London: Almark, 1971). *It is also a classic compilation on the armies at Waterloo. Lots of black-and-white drawings and commentaries about the regiments. This author was also the publisher of "The Huber Plates – The British Army," from which many further details are presented.*
13. Pericoli, Ugo, and Glover, Michael, 1815 – The Armies at Waterloo (London: Sphere Books, 1973). *Handles all the armies with numerous plate, some of which show his own interpretations, with detailed commentary texts. Very detailed drawings.*
14. Reid, S., Wellington's Highlanders (Men-at-Arms No. 253). (London: Osprey, 1992).

Contemporary series on the British army, also including those by Goddard and Booth, can be studied in the uniform portal of Napoleon-Online – see the listing of all published uniform series at http://www.napoleon-online.de/uniformserien_zeitgenossen.html (last visited on 3 January 2018).

Four volumes have been published in the series
"Uniforms of the Armies of Waterloo":

- British Army from 1815, with 75 plates
- Allied Armies from 1815, with 56 plates
- Prussian Army from 1815, with 39 plates
- French Army of 1815, with 70 plates

Orders can be placed through brick-and-mortar and online bookstores.